Cambridge Elements

Elements in Public Policy
edited by
M. Ramesh
National University of Singapore (NUS)
Michael Howlett
Simon Fraser University, British Columbia
Xun WU
Hong Kong University of Science and Technology (Guangzhou)
Judith Clifton
University of Cantabria
Eduardo Araral
National University of Singapore (NUS)

ARTIFICIAL INTELLIGENCE AND PUBLIC POLICY

Fernando Filgueiras
Federal University of Goiás and National School of Public Administration

CAMBRIDGE
UNIVERSITY PRESS

CAMBRIDGE
UNIVERSITY PRESS

Shaftesbury Road, Cambridge CB2 8EA, United Kingdom

One Liberty Plaza, 20th Floor, New York, NY 10006, USA

477 Williamstown Road, Port Melbourne, VIC 3207, Australia

314–321, 3rd Floor, Plot 3, Splendor Forum, Jasola District Centre,
New Delhi – 110025, India

103 Penang Road, #05–06/07, Visioncrest Commercial, Singapore 238467

Cambridge University Press is part of Cambridge University Press & Assessment, a department of the University of Cambridge.

We share the University's mission to contribute to society through the pursuit of education, learning and research at the highest international levels of excellence.

www.cambridge.org
Information on this title: www.cambridge.org/9781009572231

DOI: 10.1017/9781009572248

© Fernando Filgueiras 2025

This publication is in copyright. Subject to statutory exception and to the provisions of relevant collective licensing agreements, no reproduction of any part may take place without the written permission of Cambridge University Press & Assessment.

When citing this work, please include a reference to the DOI 10.1017/9781009572248

First published 2025

A catalogue record for this publication is available from the British Library

ISBN 978-1-009-57223-1 Hardback
ISBN 978-1-009-57222-4 Paperback
ISSN 2398-4058 (online)
ISSN 2514-3565 (print)

Cambridge University Press & Assessment has no responsibility for the persistence or accuracy of URLs for external or third-party internet websites referred to in this publication and does not guarantee that any content on such websites is, or will remain, accurate or appropriate.

For EU product safety concerns, contact us at Calle de José Abascal, 56, 1°, 28003 Madrid, Spain, or email eugpsr@cambridge.org

Artificial Intelligence and Public Policy

Elements in Public Policy

DOI: 10.1017/9781009572248
First published online: December 2025

Fernando Filgueiras
Federal University of Goiás and National School of Public Administration

Author for correspondence: Fernando Filgueiras, fernandofilgueiras@ufg.br

Abstract: In a global landscape increasingly shaped by technology, artificial intelligence (AI) is emerging as a disruptive force, redefining not only our daily lives but also the very essence of governance. This Element delves deeply into the intricate relationship between AI and the policy process, unraveling how this technology is reshaping the formulation, implementation, and advice of public policies, as well as influencing the structures and actors involved. Policy science was based on practice knowledge that guided the actions of policymakers. However, the rise of AI introduces an unprecedented sociotechnical reengineering, changing the way knowledge is produced and used in government. Artificial intelligence in public policy is not about transferring policy to machines but about a fundamental change in the construction of knowledge, driven by a hybrid intelligence that arises from the interaction between humans and machines.

This Element also has a video abstract:
www.cambridge.org/EPPO_Filgueiras_abstract

Keywords: artificial intelligence; governance; policy formulation; policy implementation; institutions; knowledge; learning

© Fernando Filgueiras 2025

ISBNs: 9781009572231 (HB), 9781009572224 (PB), 9781009572248 (OC)
ISSNs: 2398-4058 (online), 2514-3565 (print)

Contents

1 Introduction   1

2 Policy Process, Knowledge, and AI   3

3 AI Instruments in the Policy Process   12

4 Modeling a Disruptive Policy Cycle with AI   28

5 Governing AI in the Policy Cycle   46

6 Concluding Remarks   57

References   61

1 Introduction

In embarking on this work, our goal is to understand how and why artificial intelligence (AI) provides a sociotechnical reengineering of public policy and changes policy practice. In the same vein, this Element analyzes the consequences and challenges of disruptive changes infused by AI in the policy process and the requirements of new modes of governance. As a disruptive technology, AI directly impacts how public policy is developed within government organizations. Although a controversial and poorly defined concept, AI is an interdisciplinary field of research that involves computer science, engineering, mathematics, and an entire range of applied sciences. Our objective is to analyze how AI transforms policy science into a disruptive path that requires new standards of governance and control. Thus, addressing the consequences of AI in the practice of public policy requires navigating interdisciplinarity and considering both technical and political elements surrounding this technology.

The integration of AI into public policy happens after the changes emerged with digital governance. The digitalization of governments has meant that public services and processes have been transferred to machines. The concept of digital transformation is a process of institutional change related to the adoption of digital technologies (Vial, 2019). What epitomizes this approach is the role that digitization and digitalization play in bringing about institutional change. Digitization is to transform information into a computable object, allowing information to be converted into data and that it can be stored and communicated by machines. Digitalization refers to adopting sociotechnical methods to adopt digitizing techniques to improve social and institutional contexts, making it possible to optimize various policy domains. Digitization and digitalization comprise the main points of digital transformation, not only implying a logic of costs but of institutional changes (Anthony Jr, 2020).

The emergence of AI in government has benefited from institutional transformations within the government as the digitalization of services advances toward a conception of digital government. Algorithms have become integral to the institutionalization of public services and policies (Mendonça, Filgueiras & Almeida, 2023). Digital governments have enabled the collection of large volumes of data, produced quickly and structured into different layers, about citizens, processes, public services, and locations. Digital governments have promoted important sociotechnical changes. These practical changes occur because they not only transpose policy elements to machines but also transform the entire construction of knowledge that sets in motion the actions of policymakers. What is distinctive about the changes established by AI is that it transforms the epistemic action of policymakers. Policymakers build practical knowledge about policy on innovative bases supported by a hybrid intelligence that emerges from interactions between humans and machines. Unlike previous sociotechnical changes, the integration of AI into public policy produces a transformation at the core of practice because it is embedded in knowledge production and related government interventions.

AI in the public sector should not be conceived simply as an automation tool. Although it may have this character, the integration of AI in the public sector is deeper because its real impact lies in the transformation of policy work. According to a report by the Alan Turing Institute, generative AI, used merely as a tool for automating public services, increases public sector productivity by approximately 5%. However, the real transformation of AI in the public sector, in its various facets, lies in the way AI augments and changes the experience of policymakers, altering work practices and knowledge construction (Hashem et al., 2025). A similar result is found by Acemoglu (2024), when he analyzes the field of industry.

Governments also see the utility of AI, and they are engaged in this process of social reengineering, shifting all their sociotechnical instruments. The scope and speed with which AI is becoming embedded in the public policy process is reforming the organizational and political structures by which government action is shaped to impact society. Governments are gradually adopting AI, producing silent, incremental, and effective reforms to produce changes in the structure of knowledge and government agencies. Understanding how and why AI produces changes at the roots of public policy becomes central to the constitution of policy science. The original imagery of the policy science field is of a public policy based on knowledge and the constitution of professional discipline within public organizations. At present, we are experiencing disruptive changes that imply new ways of doing, experimenting, and reasoning to act in the public sphere. Making new sociotechnical instruments available, such as AI, means producing new ways for humans to think and act to solve different public problems. But how are these new ways impacting the policy process? What are the disruptions, for better or worse? And how can we best harness the possibilities of AI as an enabler of positive transformation?

To understand more about the impact and potential of AI in this regard, we start from the premise that policy science is undergoing disruptive changes in the epistemic structure of the field. This implies new patterns of action that organize innovative practices and novel ways of understanding problems and solutions for public policy. This process of social reengineering is based on a philosophy centered on knowledge as information, and on information as a central mechanism for constituting agency (Floridi, 2013). AI is a central element in changing the roots of policy science, altering the conditions of agency in society. At the heart of this process of social reengineering is how AI transforms power relations. In many ways, AI performs the allocation of societal resources, such as health care, social welfare resources, housing, and visas (Eubanks, 2018). AI's political impact is creating automatic authorities that exercise power more efficiently and concentratedly (Lazar, 2024). In this vein, the impact of AI on policy is enormous because it alters the frameworks of human choices by dynamically creating options for people, creating new options, nudging behavior, or forcing options. For example, predictive policing systems frame the choices of police officers who act according to the recommendations of a system built with data. These recommendations change the situations in which police officers act by creating scripts for action based on data (Mendonça, Filgueiras & Almeida, 2023).

In reviewing the literature and presenting our findings, we organize the Element into five additional sections. Section 2 produces the relationship between traditional knowledge and new emerging modes of knowledge with AI in policy cycle. This section also considers elements for a general framework of change. Section 3 deals with the concept of AI, its techniques, and developments in policy cycle as policy instruments. We want to understand how AI modifies the policy process because it modifies decision-making and tasks. In Section 4, we discuss how AI's integration into the policy process implies an overlapping of data and systems modeling across all stages of the policy cycle, creating new activities based on instrument constituencies and new practices of policy analysis and advisory. Section 5 summarizes AI governance challenges central to the policy process. Finally, we conclude by pointing out how the changes introduced by AI in public policy transform the foundations of policy science and its dialogue with society.

2 Policy Process, Knowledge, and AI

When Lasswell laid the foundations of policy science, he synthesized a scientific and professional perspective on this field of knowledge. The scientific perspective lies in the fact that public policy is problem-solving and that the connection between problems and solutions requires specific knowledge that mobilizes and encourages a particular pattern of decision-makers' agency in the policy process. Policy actors' action is the empirical object of policy science, so that the action dilemmas, perspectives, and outcomes can be understood and synthesized into theoretical knowledge. On the other hand, according to Lasswell, public policy involves a professional and technical practice that mobilizes this knowledge in a practical way to build solutions. Thus, policy science, according to Lasswell, is "knowledge of the policy process and the relevance of knowledge in the policy process" (Lasswell, 1970, p. 3).

Armed with this understanding, in this section we explore how AI, as opposed to traditional knowledge gathering, supplies information, and how it may impact the policy process. To have a broader understanding of the potential implications, we discuss what a general framework of change could entail.

2.1 Policy Process and Knowledge

In looking at policy process, three characteristics of the field of policy science are essential. First, policy science deals with applied knowledge, and it is oriented toward problem-solving. Second, this knowledge requires contextuality. Third, the knowledge produced by policy science is interdisciplinary (De Leon, 1981). Understood as specialized, applied, and interdisciplinary knowledge, work with public policy involves the government's epistemic agency to solve problems. Placing policy science as an epistemic agency means that policy decision-makers mobilize their action based on knowledge of problems and the positive connection of these problems with knowledge about solutions. Problems, represented through information, mean inputs for policymakers' actions, constituting a solution or outputs of the government agency in organizational contexts. Working with public policy involves agents understanding a problem and acting to build a solution and new knowledge about policy outcomes and dilemmas. The distinctive characteristic of policy science is to constitute applied knowledge that connects public problems to solutions constructed in contexts of collective decision-making.

Public policy embeds professional and technical knowledge and constant learning to create solutions to public problems (Heclo, 1974; Dunlop & Radaelli, 2020). The epistemic action of public policy professionals is shaped and infused by an interdisciplinary practical knowledge that enables them to reason and design solutions. Knowledge in policy science is essential because, in many situations, it organizes how policymakers and managers select a purpose, create means of action, and diffuse policy objectives. The actors' actions lead to discussions about policy science's theoretical framework. This theoretical framework leads to reflection on different models of understanding the construction of knowledge and its practical application by professionals from governments and interest groups.

Public policy is an applied, interdisciplinary, and professional-oriented knowledge field. The public policy profession occurs in the organizational dimension. For example, the garbage can model criticizes the policy cycle's conception by pointing out that knowledge of solutions precedes knowledge of problems, shaping decision-making as complex, infused by bounded rationality, and driven by fluid participation. Cohen, March, and Olsen (1972) recognize that decision-making, policy formulation, and implementation adhere to the phenomenon of organizations. Organizations are the ones that fulfill public policy's purpose and shape professional practice. Policymakers understand that, within organizations, public policies are artifacts to solve problems that involve professional practice within an organizational context and create public values (Barzelay, 2019).

Public policy's professional practice involves solving problems, which requires coordinated activity to mobilize multiple knowledge domains. Organizations make decisions, and policymakers design artifacts in their context to solve problems. Public policy is designed in organizational contexts, from which professionals engender a complex chain of interactions driven by analysis, prototyping, testing, evaluation, and decision-making (Simon, 1970; Howlett, 2019). In this dimension, public policy is a function of practical knowledge absorbed or produced by policymakers' experience within organizations, which shapes a professional discipline.

Public policy relies on professional knowledge shaped in diverse political contexts, grounded in a conception of knowledge that combines scientific perspectives with practical political applications. Thus, social science influences the practice of public policy, while the practice of public policy also influences social science. Knowledge in public policy is politically shaped and constitutes an element of practical action in defense of a collective purpose (Weiss, 1979).

The epistemic challenge means understanding the public policy process – that is, how knowledge of problems translates into knowledge of solutions to accomplish a purpose. For many analysts, the policy process is linear between problems and solutions, respecting rational policymaking and aimed at optimization (Braybrooke & Lindblom, 1963). On the other hand, there are those in which the policy process is non-linear, in which policies depend on political, ideational, or psychological factors because of the idea of bounded rationality (Simon, 1947; Lindblom, 1959). Finally, there is an intermediate perspective of rationality. Knowledge is a factor that organizes decisions rather than precisely making rationality. Mixed scanning, for example, works with the idea that policy decisions are not linear, but that knowledge is a rationalizing factor for actors' strategies in different situations involving collective decision-making (Etzioni, 1968).

Research is conducted over a given period or based on past dynamics to overcome the problems of irrationality or limitations. As Baumgartner and Jones (2015) point out, information plays an essential role in the policy cycle.

The dynamics of policy agendas, for example, are unpredictable and complex and are inherently difficult to forecast. However, the production of knowledge is central to the policy process. Governance is a problem of information: getting it (or restricting it), ensuring it is reliable (which sometimes means reliably consistent with one's priors), and acting on it. Political institutions are seen through this lens, focusing less on representation, partisanship, or organized groups than on information processing (Baumgartner & Jones, 2015). Increasing the volume and quality of information, therefore, represents crucial elements for improving the performance of public policy in society.

Knowledge mechanisms, their artifacts, and their usefulness in the policy process define many aspects of what we can call policy science. Conceived from a scientific and professional perspective, within organizations, public policy involves the interdisciplinary connection between knowledge and practice, thus shaping action within governments. Disruptions, however, form new perspectives and changes that transform knowledge production and practice. We are experiencing a gradual disruption of public policy practice due to changes in the information regime and the emergence of digital technologies such as AI (Dunleavy & Margetts, 2024). The disruption lies in AI transforming the epistemic roots of policy science and changing the everyday practice of public policy. The framework we work with in this Element is that AI changes the epistemic bases of government action in society by conceiving information through data and agency effects through complex algorithms that form AI-based systems. In the next section, we clarify the terms of the epistemic change.

2.2 Epistemic Changes and AI Integration in Policymaking

Regardless of the types of policy knowledge and decision-making, policy science's epistemology changes over time. Today, the idea prevails that we live in a disruptive world in which innovative technologies change the epistemic roots of policy science (Hartley & Kuecker, 2022). This disruptive world is an interesting perspective to portray a moment when the practice of public policy changes radically. Traditionally, policy advice and learning sources are consultancies, political parties, academia, and civil society organizations, which select, curate, and promote problems (Craft & Howlett, 2013; Craft & Halligan, 2020).

Currently, we are dealing with an epistemic change that occurs with the volume of information expanding on social life's diverse aspects. The volume is ballooning because of the data amassed, shared, and processed in everyday life. First, information and evidence abound on problems due to large volumes of data (Kitchin, 2014). Second, there is an expansion of knowledge sources that change policy advice dynamics (Safaei & Longo, 2024). In addition to consultancies, parties, academia, and civil society, the volume of information is expanding, whether it is the result of social media or expert systems that structure digital governments (Giest, 2017).

Although there are multiple perspectives on how knowledge influences policy decisions and tasks, the idea of having a greater volume of information is a vital factor for policy rationalization and organization (Baumgartner & Jones, 2015). Digital technologies have long played an essential role in the policy process. Since the foundations of policy science, computational systems have activated an imaginary of qualification and rationalization of the policy process through the dimension of professional techniques. Lasswell's imagination, for example, is constructing a professional perspective of public policy mobilized by scientific knowledge, in which problems and evidence guide the work of policy analysts and can be instrumented by computational technologies (Lasswell, 1970).

In Lasswell's argument, the policy work, guided by "computerized" information, is essential in a scientific nature and in constructing a technical image of its professionals. Positive public policy, as Lasswell argues, has data and information and communication technologies as the basis for building evidence and positive government action in society. Furthermore, cybernetic conceptions of government place a vital element in data (Hood & Margetts, 2007). The role that information plays in the policy process is part of a cybernetic conception of government action, in which actors understand the environment, react to information about the environment, make decisions, and establish value on the consequences of their decisions and actions implemented over time (Hood & Margetts, 2007; Peters, 2012). This cybernetic conception of government has been introduced previously and coincides with AI's emergence and construction (Samuel, 1962; Deutsch, 1963; Schwember, 1977). Currently, the disruption caused by AI in public policy is the result of changes in societies' information regimes and the advancement of technologies capable of processing this information to generate knowledge and practice (Dunleavy & Margetts, 2024).

This idea of strengthening policy analysts' techniques and profession through digital technologies was reactivated by the possibility of using digital technologies throughout the public policy process. The use of blockchain to rearrange public organizations (Clifton & Pal, 2022), the Internet of Things (IoT) to collect data and information in urban space (Chetfield & Reddick, 2019), the use of large volumes of data in the policy process (Giest, 2017), and the use of robots in public health, industry, and transportation (Willems et al., 2022) are examples of how digital technologies are becoming pervasive in the government domain. Digital technologies in government aim to strengthen policy science and create a new dynamic of more technical and evidence-oriented professional practices. This imagination became hyped with AI's reinvention (Filgueiras, 2022a). More than reimagining the possibilities of applying AI to public policy, this technology transforms the roots of knowledge.

In all the main theoretical traditions of policy science, AI transforms the possibilities and frames of policy creation. In positivist perspectives, AI has established transformations in the way evidence is produced and influences the policy process. Because large volumes of data are analyzed by machines and have practical consequences, the use of AI constitutes a new arrangement for the construction and use of information, implying changes in the positive policy (Newman & Mintrom, 2023). Policy analysis is what professional public servants do when they use information to create advice for policy decision makers (Wilson, 2009). AI transforms the analysis of evidence, accelerating the production of information and changing advice practices. From a positivist framework, AI generates scientific knowledge about policies, as it is based on formal statistical models that scientifically predict and advise courses of action for different actors in policymaking contexts.

From a critical policy analysis, public policy is analyzed through narratives and discourses that focus on power dynamics, social structures, and the ways policies shape and are shaped by social and political contexts (Fischer, 2016). In many situations, the use of AI shapes synthetic social and political contexts. Algorithms shape and are shaped by discourses, creating frames of practical action by humans (Mendonça, Filgueiras & Almeida, 2023). The use of generative AI in urban policies, for example, shapes synthetic contexts that boost anticipatory forms of governance, through which state actors seek to predict the future and strategically intervene in the present. As Cugurullo and Xu (2025) point out, the use of City Brain, a generative AI, enable policymakers to manage multiple urban domains, including transport, safety, health, and environmental monitoring. City Brain uses large language models (LLMs) to generate visions of urban futures: visions that are in turn used by policymakers to generate new urban policies. The use of this generative AI creates frames and discourses for action, creating new risks and perspectives for the formulation of urban policies (Cugurullo & Xu, 2025).

Another example is how generative AI transforms the actions of low-skilled workers, adding more emotional discursive layers to automated work with AI. Automation is a limited conception in terms of discursive production. Low-skilled workers are unable to embed their own problems in the larger social context of generative AI's impact on the labor market, let alone to politicize these problems. The impacts of new emerging patterns of interaction between humans and machines create the need for policies aimed at adapting workers to the context of AI (Oder & Béland, 2025).

In a critical vein, the integration of AI into public policy requires a more cautious approach since the context in which AI is shaped by global asymmetries, uncertainties about the values that are introduced into algorithms, and how the practices that emerge are contingent and shaped by interactions between humans and machines (Paul, 2022). In all these situations, AI transforms knowledge about public policy, which automates and expands analytical capacities, but without the backdrop of human oversight.

The integration of AI and public policy has more specific implications regarding epistemic issues. Policymakers' actions change in response to the presence of new artifacts that produce and expand knowledge about policy solutions and problems. Epistemic agency refers to an individual's capacity to form, revise, and justify beliefs and to participate in knowledge-related activities (Scholosser, 2019). Epistemic agency in public policy emerges from epistemic communities that share knowledge within a specific area to build expertise (Dunlop, 2017). In public policy, epistemic agency refers to the capacity of policymakers to manage their beliefs and construct knowledge. Policy epistemic agency refers to the construction of vectors of practical learning within the context of epistemic communities aimed at utilizing techniques and technologies that shape practical action. In this sense, epistemic agency concerns the analytical capacities of policymakers to understand problems and propose solutions. Analytical capacities encompass a set of skills for processing data and evidence and proposing solutions related to various policy functions (Howlett, 2015). AI amplifies analytical capacities, as it shapes and revises policymakers' beliefs and actions in unexplored directions.

AI promises a disruptive change in the practice when integrated into public policy. On the one hand, AI reshapes the public sector's entire organization, modifying public agents' capacities, proposing a more vertical governance style of policy sectors, and the horizontal allocation of power and functions between organizations through state integration, common capacity, and a needs-based convergence of services (Dunleavy & Margetts, 2024). On the other hand, AI provides a new epistemology and patterns of epistemic action (Coeckelbergh, 2023; Floridi, 2023a), reflected in new analysis and new public policy practices by its professionals (Safaei & Longo, 2024; Taeihagh, 2025; Jaidka et al., 2025). Thus, AI allows policymakers to modify their knowledge and reasoning and think about government action in a complex and different world, with a new order of problems and innovative technologies to shape solutions.

For example, Open AI, an owner of ChatGPT, has a trained and customized policy advisor chat, which promises to do the following:

- break down policy proposals, legislation, or regulations to assess their potential impacts, benefits, and drawbacks;
- offer insights on how to approach policy challenges, engage stakeholders, and navigate the policy-making process effectively;
- identify opportunities for innovation within public services and suggest ways to implement new ideas;
- help understand and interpret data relevant to policy issues, including economic indicators, public health statistics, or educational outcomes; and
- provide examples of successful policies from other regions or sectors that could be adapted or learned.[1]

This solution promises to replace policymakers' knowledge practice, constituting another advisory standard from which they learn about problems and solutions, create cognitive structures, and reason about their actions in the government organizational context. Furthermore, it changes the entire practice of policy advice and learning (Henman, 2018; Safaei & Longo, 2024).

AI represents a knowledge instrument that changes practices and interacts with humans to solve different problems. In public policy, AI goes beyond the conventional classification of policy instruments. AI is a pervasive instrument that can produce nodality, regulation, organization, and define fiscal management mechanisms. For this reason, AI is beyond the digitalization process. AI is not just an automation engine. It falls beyond the taxonomy of substantive and procedural digital instruments (Howlett et al., 2025) and should be considered a pervasive knowledge instrument throughout the policy cycle.

Hood and Margetts (2007) classify policy instruments into authority, treasury, nodality, and organization. The arrangement and mix of instruments to achieve a policy objective depend on an information regime. Epistemic communities produce information, which is an essential input for public policy design (Dunlop, 2016, Capano & Malandrino, 2022). AI modifies the epistemic regime of public policy in dimension of inputs, throughputs, and outputs, augmenting and aligning information through technology (König & Wenzelburguer, 2020; Dunleavy & Margetts, 2024). AI represents an epistemic instrument that overlaps other policy instruments, modifying the dynamics of policy design. For instance, AI helps policymakers change

---

[1] https://community.openai.com/t/policy-advisor-custom-gpt-for-public-policy-professionals/702969/1.

nodality, creating more direct forms of communication between government and society (Margetts & John, 2024). Similarly, AI transforms the way governments collect and administer taxes, changing all instruments of treasury (Mökander & Schoereder, 2024). AI also transforms public organizations by introducing new patterns of agency and organizational functions (Neumann, Guirguis & Steiner, 2022). Finally, AI transforms the regulatory practices of governments (Ghosh, Saini & Barad, 2025).

In other words, AI shifts the epistemic regime of public policy. Epistemic regimes are stable arrangements of practices of knowledge production and social structures (Knorr-Cetina, 1999). Policy analysts frame the policy practices from epistemic regimes. AI changes the practices of knowledge construction about public policy, creating a new layer of complexity in public policy practice. AI is both absorbed as a new practice in policy science and results in the framing of professional practices of policy analysts. By changing these practices, AI transforms the institutional arrangements that guide the agency of professionals in political contexts. The above example of ChatGPT acting as a policy analyst is a construction of this perspective of change. If widely adopted by governments, this large language model could produce knowledge in an increased and rapid manner, with prospects of meeting the demands of humans related to a policy field.

An illustrative example of this process is how the Intergovernmental Panel on Climate Change (IPCC) has successfully laid a baseline of scientific facts for global discussions on climate action. Based on multiple layers and AI algorithms, the dashboard modulates complex scientific information about climate change, infusing policymakers with a new knowledge structure that modifies policy practice (Cowls et al., 2023). AI applied at the IPCC provides climate modeling, prediction and simulations, and the design of catastrophic scenarios, as well as chatbots to expand the communication of IPCC data and reports and monitor government actions. In addition to providing information about climate data, AI applied in climate change supports studies on past environmental change around displacement hotspots and delivers future projections to inform adaptation measures and anticipatory action for integration in humanitarian programming. Similarly, AI can support disaster prevention, tracking pollution, and building climate-resilient agrifood systems that are more efficient, sustainable, and adaptable to climate change challenges. Within the practices of climate policy, data and information are modeled to predict and simulate scenarios that guide government action in innovative areas. AI organizes different climate policy challenges. AI climate policy implies new recommendations for practical action taken by policymakers and bureaucrats (Muccione et al., 2024).

The IPCC and the embedded AI have changed the structure of knowledge and action of policymakers around the world, providing new patterns of political disputes framed by the possibilities of global warming. The IPCC illustrates how AI, by modifying the information regime, modifies political action in different directions depending on the framing resulting from the complex work with data. The AI systems embedded in the IPCC represent complex knowledge instruments, thus altering the dynamics of environmental policy. In all these situations, predictions, simulations, and AI modeling modify policymakers' epistemic action in the context of climate policies. First, climate change policy requires global negotiation and outreach, strategic partnerships, and implementation processes beyond issues internal to the nation-state. Second, climate change policies require the creation of networks to adapt global infrastructure, intensely shifting production and consumption chains. Finally, climate change requires policymakers to implement mitigation actions, which involve direct organizational changes in bureaucratic agencies and infusing behavioral changes in society. Mitigation actions require new formats, knowledge, and instruments for policy design (Braunerhjelm & Hepburn, 2023). AI-generated knowledge in climate policy frames political disputes, in which policy knowledge is challenged by conspiracy theories that put political action beliefs at stake (van Prooijen et al., 2025).

These changes in the epistemic action of policymakers, encouraged by an AI-based system, mean that AI is providing new sociotechnical standards for public policy and has consequences in society. A sociotechnical conception of AI in public policy means how human agents interact with this technology and produce new action patterns in complex organizational contexts. AI creates a new context for knowledge production and action that infuses policy changes in dimensions of government and its institutions. Understanding what AI is and the framework needed to think about its consequences is essential in the composition of AI in the policy process. Furthermore, changes in the information regime and the production of knowledge through AI in public policy require a critical view regarding their placement in the policy cycle. AI, as we will see in the next section, brings opportunities and risks to the policy cycle, assuming an ambiguous character in relation to the sociotechnical reengineering of public policies.

3 AI Instruments in the Policy Process

To have a deeper grasp on how policymakers may harness AI in a meaningful way, it is important to consider the roles it can or cannot play. This requires a firm understanding of what AI actually is, thereby shedding light on AI's capabilities in terms of how it may modify decisions and tasks as part of the policy process.

As we demonstrated in the previous section, the integration of AI into the policy cycle changes the foundation for knowledge construction and, in turn, policy practice. In this section, we will take a step further, examining the various technical elements of AI to support the thesis that the integration of AI into the policy cycle entails the configuration of hybrid intelligence in policymaking. What is innovative about the integration of AI into the policy cycle is that it creates, in the context of governments, a hybrid intelligence that changes the dynamics of policymaking. Hybrid intelligence integrates collective human and machine intelligence in a structured way to perform a series of tasks (Moradi et al., 2019). Hybrid intelligence enables the expansion of collective intelligence and the development of a concept of human-driven AI (Verhulst, 2018). In public policy, this hybrid form of intelligence implies new dynamics and conceptions that create new dilemmas for policies shaped together with AI (König & Wenzelburguer, 2020; Ahn & Chen, 2022). Hybrid intelligence is designed with general purposes to enable interactions between humans and machines to deepen the construction of knowledge (Liu, Tang & Collard, 2025).

Defining AI is essential to understanding how this technology, in interaction with humans, produces changes in the policy process because it alters the conditions of human agency in institutional contexts. In many cases, AI deinstitutionalizes and reinstitutionalizes elements of the policy process by altering the conditions of agency of policymakers. In addition, it is essential to understand how artificial intelligence creates new practices or reproduces old patterns, and is not a solution based on "one size fits all".

3.1 What Is AI?

Artificial intelligence is not a thing or a singular technology. AI does not have a precise concept in specialized literature (Wang, 2019). The conceptual bases of AI are in machine intelligence to perform a task or solve a problem, which can vary according to the concept of intelligence (Russell, 2019). AI is a computational technology that imitates human intelligence but can vary depending on how intelligence is conceived. The philosophical foundation behind AI development is imitation (Turing, 1950).

It is important to emphasize that AI can be deconstructed in two dimensions. The first has to do with the difficult concept of intelligence. If machines imitate human intelligence, the first step is to define what intelligence means. The concept of intelligence focuses on human agency and understanding the drivers of action in different contexts to solve problems. Humans are intelligent not because they have intellectual abilities but because they can intervene to achieve a particular purpose. Intelligence can be many different things. Intelligence can mean the idea of rationality, considering the ability of humans to realize their preferences in each context and maximize the greatest possible utility (Simon, 1957).

The concept of preferences is based on the premise that humans know perfectly well what they want and that they will choose an optimal option in many situations. Intelligence can also be considered bounded rationality, which implies that human action is not based on perfect preferences but on heuristics that constitute an informational shortcut that leads humans to decide on the most satisfactory option and not the optimal option (Kahneman, 2003). Intelligence also can mean the human capacity to learn and form cognitive structures that allow them to perform in the world (Russell & Norvig, 2010) or perhaps the capacity for abstraction. Abstraction is a crucial function that enables humans to perform different tasks (Minsky, 1985). Intelligence can be structured thinking, in which humans understand, plan, and reason to achieve specific goals and solve problems (Markram, 2006). In a more simplified conception, human intelligence derives from the fact that humans are machines for constructing patterns and storing those patterns as information to act (Kahneman, 2003).

There is no need here to define intelligence exhaustively, but this concept creates initial difficulties. Intelligence is a human capacity to act based on abstraction, logic, understanding, self-awareness, learning, emotional knowledge, reasoning, planning, creativity, critical thinking, and problem-solving. In all these definitions, intelligence means some practical knowledge aimed directly at action in the world through social interactions and exchanges (Goldman, 2003). Intelligence involves how humans infer information and construct knowledge to adapt their behavior to the environment through exchanges that exist in social interactions (Simon, 1983; Goldman, 2003). Intelligence presupposes a capacity of everyone. However, it also has a collective dimension established in meanings, common actions, and shared political knowledge. The collective dimension of intelligence is, by definition, a political dimension (Landemore, 2012).

The other side of the AI concept is that we have the issue of artificiality. According to Simon (1970), this dimension of artificial entails the idea that systems interact with humans to achieve a particular purpose. Here, we point out an essential premise for understanding AI. What is different about AI systems is that they are in permanent interaction with humans through computational interfaces designed for human affairs (Cross & Ramsey, 2021). When interacting with humans, machines incorporate different ranges of human problems to solve them and perform tasks (Reid & Gibert, 2022). Systems only have a particular form and behavior because they adapt to their environment to accomplish objectives or purposes in interaction with humans. Thus, human artifacts, in terms of their behavior, are artificial. Simon (1970) characterizes an artificial system as an interface between internal and external environments. These environments belong to the "natural science" domain, but the interface that connects them is the "science of artificial" domain, which comprises an interdisciplinary dynamic that converges different forms of knowledge for constructing a given artifact. When an artificial system successfully adapts, its behavior mainly shows the external environment's shape and reveals little about the internal environment's structure or mechanisms (Simon, 1970).

We can construct a general concept of AI using these two dimensions. *Artificial intelligence is a computer system capable of operating, in interaction with humans, different techniques to calculate, predict, and simulate courses of action from large volumes of data to support humans in decision-making and carrying out tasks.* This definition embeds five essential elements of AI, especially if we consider this definition for applications focused on public policy.

1. AI depends on large amounts of data to generate analysis, learning, reasoning, and action (Kitchin, 2014; DeSouza, 2017; Dunleavy, 2016).
2. Different AI techniques start from the premise of imitating human intelligence performed by algorithms (Russell & Norvig, 2010). As we have seen, intelligence has many definitions, each of which implies diverse ways of thinking and reasoning to solve a problem.
3. AI systems depend on interfaces through which machines interact with humans (Simon, 1995).
4. AI systems are epistemic when processing large volumes of data to support decision-making and task accomplishment (McCarthy, 1981).
5. An AI system's constitution has a purpose; therefore, this system intends to affect agency issues directly and can carry out some action (Barandiaran, Di Paolo & Rohde, 2009; Tomasello, 2022).

Because AI is many different things and not a singular technology, the label "artificial intelligence" must be understood in its epistemic and not ontological dimension (Alvarado, 2023). AI is a field of research and knowledge, shaped by different techniques. Among the best known, machine learning is an AI technique in which computer systems calculate a specific output from learning vectors calculated in a structured database for training. In other words, they are algorithms that let the machine learn from the training database and produce an output from the learned vectors (Samuel, 1959; Domingos, 2015). Algorithms shape this learning process, and it can be supervised or unsupervised. It is supervised when the machine learns from a human-categorized database. This structured database serves as supervision of the knowledge constituted by machines; it guides – or supervises – how outputs will be constructed. The other possibility is that the outputs are unsupervised. In this case, the machines calculate learning vectors autonomously and use them to create the desired outputs.

Machine learning is the main technique, but the field of AI expands into other techniques. Among them, we have ensemble learning that aggregates two or more learners (e.g., regression models or neural networks) to produce better predictions (Zhou, 2012). Deep learning is another offshoot and subfield of machine learning. Using premises from neuroscience, deep learning entails AI techniques in which multilayered neural networks are applied to simulate the complex decision-making power of the human brain (LeCun, Bengio & Hinton, 2015). Reinforcement learning focuses on decision-making by autonomous agents. It is mainly applied in robotics, where an autonomous agent is any system that can make decisions and act in response to its environment independent of direct instruction by a human user (Sutton & Barto, 2018).

Within machine learning techniques, different applications exist, such as natural language processing (NLP); within NLP techniques, there are large language models (LLMs). LLMs are embedded in systems such as ChatGPT and Gemini, enabling machine interaction with humans. LLM is a computational language processing system designed to generate sequences of words, codes, or other data (more recently, images) from an input sequence called "prompt" and processed by transformer algorithms (Eisenstein, 2019). Another set of techniques is AI systems based on computer vision, which use images or videos from various sources to train systems that perform tasks that depend on image recognition. Facial recognition applications in public safety (Chen, Surette & Shah, 2021) or autonomous cars, for instance, use computer vision techniques to perform tasks and decision-making (Padmaja et al., 2023).

Finally, we have large action models (LAM) at the forefront of AI advancement and disruption with AI agents. This AI technique combines elements of neural networks inspired by brain architecture with aspects of symbolic AI, which focuses on logic and symbols (Yang, Wu & Jiang, 2007; Zhuo et al., 2010). This fusion of techniques helps LAMs capture and model the complex relationships between user intentions and the actions performed by AI.

In short, AI systems are designed and implemented with large volumes of data, different algorithms, and computational power embedded in interfaces that shape human-machine interactions. Data represents numbers, images, texts, and any element from which we construct information that can be collected, stored, and shared in critical infrastructures (Kitchin, 2014). Algorithms represent the "rules of the game" (Turing, 1950), from which courses of action are calculated and infused into the interaction between humans and machines (Mendonça, Filgueiras & Almeida, 2023). In many situations, algorithms are the elements that institutionalize rules and procedures, shaping human behavior and choices through diverse interfaces. Finally, AI systems are produced from large machines that amplify computational power in data storage and processing. Computer power is about the computing infrastructure where data are collected and processed, and algorithms perform complex calculations. This infrastructure is typically shared by cloud models that can assume private, public, or hybrid ownership. This infrastructure defines many elements of AI's geopolitics (Rikap, 2021; Lehdonvirta, 2024).

The goal is for machines to discover patterns of action and generate knowledge and implications for human action from data that characterizes a given environment. In other words, AI is a tool that supports humans in building knowledge to act in increasingly complex, ambiguous, and uncertain environments. Modeling supports humans in making decisions and perform complex tasks, generating rapid knowledge and the possibility of interventions in society (Arcas, 2024). A machine becomes intelligent when it can learn how to understand – or model – its environment (Arcas, 2024). When the machine becomes able to model its environment, it generates information that defines action situations in interaction with humans, defines informational frameworks, and produces action scripts that aim to achieve an objective. Modeling is at the heart of AI, so it allows a machine to autonomously understand its environment according to models built by humans to achieve an objective.

3.2 AI as Policy Instruments

In public policy, AI defines and frames the political context, chooses political biases from input data and information, produces knowledge outcomes, and affects both the automation of tasks and human action resulting from the knowledge created (König & Wenzelburguer, 2020). Thus, when humans interact with AI to make decisions or perform various tasks, in the context of policymaking, the machine chooses the political biases of decisions and tasks performed by policymakers. In this context of policymaking with AI, several problems emerge, such as biases, transparency, and accountability (Papadakis et al., 2024). Integrating AI into public policy means creating unfamiliar problems, dilemmas, and challenges related to the interaction between the technical and political elements associated with policymaking (Taeihagh, 2025). Policymakers and analysts need to understand the technical elements of AI and the emerging challenges of incorporating this technology into the policy cycle.

We can establish different applications in policy processes by integrating AI. For example, facial recognition systems are applied to implement public security actions, systems that perform administrative tasks automatically, policy evaluation and monitoring processes, knowledge of citizens' preferences, learning, and cognition on the part of policymakers to understand problems and propose solutions (Mendonça, Filgueiras & Almeida, 2023). The essential task for integrating AI into public policy is to have large data sets and model these data to achieve a specific knowledge goal so that the machine can understand the environment and receive feedback from humans about this environment and the action.

The debate on AI is twofold. Each perspective in the debate defines the thought on AI and its social construction. In the first approach, AI is conceived as agents that decide autonomously. The first perspective is that AI means the constitution of autonomous agents. These perspectives on the AI debate have different consequences for its integration into the policy cycle. This definition, therefore, involves the fact that AI represents agents or multiagents that perform tasks and make decisions (Wang, 2019). This first frame implies thinking of AI as agents in the policy process. Thinking of AI as agents makes some sense if we consider that these agents perform actions to make decisions and carry out tasks autonomously. If AI is conceived as an agent, in the public policy cycle, it is a new actor in the decision-making process scene.

Criticism of this conception of AI agency assumes that, to have an agency, technology must make autonomous decisions. Autonomy is one of the assumptions of agency, and it is constituted controversially. The tendency to attribute autonomy to AI systems disregards that these computational systems do not have consciousness (Floridi, 2023a). Autonomy presupposes consciousness and intentionality, which obscures the idea of AI as agents or multiagents. AI is an artifact built by humans in human contexts.

This discussion is foundational in the field of AI. Since the classic work of Joseph Weizenbaum (1976), the idea of autonomy and AI's anthropomorphization has been discussed. By anthropomorphization, we refer to attributing human qualities to machines, especially emotional abilities and intentionality. Claims to avoid anthropomorphization are recurrent, especially concerning LLMs and chats (Bender et al., 2021; Coeckelbergh, 2021; Shardlow & Przybila, 2023). The fact is that within this anthropomorphization process is how AI represents systems that interact with humans to solve problems. In this process of interaction, the tendency of anthropomorphization occurs and solidifies in the human imagination.

The second perspective is to conceive these computational systems from an instrumental reason (Weizenbaum, 1976). Instruments such as computational systems provide new possibilities for the world's imaginative reengineering. Or, more specifically, in this Element, the imaginative reengineering of policy science (Lasswell, 1970). However, according to Weizenbaum, the way computational systems designers recreate the world implies the prominence of an instrumental reason. This frame conceives AI as an instrument for human action in different fields, constituting knowledge and changing the nature of human action.

In this second frame, we can conceive of AI in the policy process as an essential instrument for policy actors, in which intentionality and knowledge depend on human action in technology design (Filgueiras, 2022a). In the policy process, AI is an instrument to perform regulatory, nodal, organizational, and financial functions, altering the capacities and skills of policymakers and actors in different policy domains. AI is an epistemic instrument primarily designed, developed, and deployed for use in epistemic contexts such as policy analysis and research. AI is specifically designed, developed, and deployed to manipulate epistemic content such as data, and it is applied to do so, particularly through epistemic operations such as prediction and analysis (Alvarado, 2023).

In the context of this Element, we adopt this second perspective for two reasons. First, AI in the policy process is an epistemic instrument that supports humans in making decisions and performing various tasks. There is no reason to imagine an AI that presents intentionality. Intentionality in public policy is collectively created. Since public policy requires intentionality to define political objectives, no AI technology can define them. AI does not define these objectives independently without human intervention. Therefore, it can frame political choices and change power relations (Lazar, 2024). Second, AI in public policy involves affordances. AI can perceive an environment designed by its developers, who use affordances to represent potential actions that exist as a relationship between an agent and its environment. Applied to public policy, affordances are essential to AI design. Designers and the modeling of available data frame the affordances in AI design. The choice of these affordances means that AI systems, when applied in the policy process, do not constitute agents but instruments that support human decision-making and tasks (Maragno et al., 2023).

AI applied in public policy is a type of knowledge technology with different epistemic effects on how policymakers think, reflect, understand, or reason policy problems and solutions through interactions between humans and machines. The disruptive point of using this technology in public policy is that it produces epistemic changes in policy practice, creates new dilemmas and problems, and changes organizational dynamics from the moment that practitioners and AI-based computer systems interact to solve problems, produce analysis, and apply this knowledge to the everyday policy practice. Understanding these interactions between humans and AI systems is the next component of the analysis undertaken here.

3.3 Human–Machine Interactions and Policy

One of AI's main characteristics is that humans and machines interact to create knowledge and act to achieve a purpose. The determining factor in AI's conception is that humans and machines interact and constitute a new form of intelligence, shaped from data and institutionalized through algorithms (Mendonça, Filgueiras & Almeida, 2023). The attribution of purpose to computer-based artifacts emerges from each human action that shapes an immediate machine reaction (Turkle, 1984). Interactions between humans and machines imply an exchange of meanings based on how users instill a need and how the machine responds. The human-machine interactions create a new cognitive structure based on normative meanings, preferences, or opinions interchangeable in interactions and situated in a context for action. The postulate is that the capacity for human agency constantly reconfigures based on interaction dynamics between humans and machines (Suchman, 2007) and becomes institutionalized in response to action situations, frames, and algorithmically defined action scripts (Mendonça, Filgueiras & Almeida, 2023).

As an epistemic tool, the contemporary world lives with hybrid intelligence, driven by humans interacting with machines to solve problems (Jarrahi, Lutz & Newlands, 2022). This characteristic of hybrid intelligence is how humans interact with systems. Hybrid intelligence is essential for understanding AI's place in public policy, why AI changes the information regime and enables another action context. Humans and machines interact and create a feedback loop that transforms the epistemic conditions of public policy. In other words, humans and AI interact to develop policies through intelligence shaped by the interaction between humans and machines. Humans and machines co-evolve information, modifying the epistemic conditions of public decision-making (Pedreschi et al., 2025). Under these conditions, humans insert inputs, receive outputs, react to them by giving new inputs, and receive new outputs in a loop that alters their understanding of the environment. By modifying the understanding of the environment, AI integrated into public policy changes the conditions of policy development and its consequences for society.

AI is a general-purpose instrument for use in different policy domains and as a different means to replace other instruments. AI can perform actions to exercise nodality, authority, treasury, and organization. Furthermore, AI transforms the way policy actors will act in the policy process. A hybrid intelligence's character derives from the way AI, thought of as an instrument, changes the perceptions, reasoning, analysis, and policy work. The literature on policy instruments shows how they are not neutral because they produce specific effects regardless of the objectives pursued (Lascoumes & Le Galès, 2007). As a pervasive and general policy instrument, AI produces changes in the policy cycle, incorporating objectives defined politically by policymakers within a context of values, interests, and perspectives that shape the design of instruments and their reach in society.

For this reason, digital technologies such as AI, when integrated into public policy, use political affordances in their design. This means that the field of public policy must understand how instruments such as AI exert influence on its intended target audience (Hellström & Jacob, 2017). The effects of AI when integrated into public policy are to facilitate action and learning. The notion of affordance involves the idea that action must be understood from the possibilities made available in object world, given the agents' skills. Public policy developed with AI instruments defines the possibilities and scope of a public policy in society. AI changes the practice of public policy because this epistemic instrument defines, according to its design and modeling, the possibilities of actors in context of government action.

In different situations, humans interact with machines to design and build AI, and AI systems incorporate policy design and institutional dynamics to achieve policy objectives and augment public value. The disruptive point of AI for public policy is that these interactions between humans and machines change policy process dynamics, which are now carried out by other means, with different consequences and new epistemics for policy science. Interactions are constituted from meanings, and the sociological premise is that individuals interact by how they interpret these meanings, which they attribute based on norms (Blumer, 1986). These meanings are institutionalized through responses to action situations, frames, and action scripts that define motivations for human action based on algorithmically created knowledge (Mendonça, Filgueiras & Almeida, 2023).

Interactions between humans and machines in the policy process will manifest in two dimensions. According to Daugherty and Wilson (2018), these dimensions involve human dynamics in designing AI, on the one hand, and the way AI assists humans, on the other. This interactive dynamic between humans and machines depends on human inputs so that machines react to them and reciprocate feedback. Interactions between humans and machines are at the heart of AI, sparking discussions about machine intelligence (Searle, 1980; Simon & Eisenstadt, 2002). Reciprocal feedback shapes new formats of knowledge, altering human action in society. Specifically in the field of public policy, interactions between humans and machines change the bases of the epistemic action of actors involved in the policy process because AI, in addition to being fed by diverse data, incorporates into its design political affordances that define the possibilities and alternatives of humans.

AI in public policy are systems that react to inputs posed by policy actors. The meanings attributed to this interaction between humans and machines in the policy process are still unknown. However, some clues exist in emerging experimental research. In the work by Alon-Barkat and Busuioc (2023), AI's adoption in public policy is driven by bureaucrats' and decision-makers' perceptions and stereotypes when they receive policy advice automatically. In other words, systems' ability to augment data and information and constitute stereotypical policy advice based on the group's biases engages AI adoption in government (Alon-Barkat & Busuioc, 2023). Human-machine interactions shape the meanings in the policy process, infusing ideas, norms, preferences, and perspectives that reinforce the biases of decision-makers and implementers. AI is dependent on the quality of the dataset, which may contain biases, omissions of excluded populations, or intentional designs toward certain target audiences. According to the experiment conducted by Alon-Barkat and Busuioc (2023), policy decision-makers are more interested in the outcome and realize these results through their own biases.

In the policy process, these dimensions occur in the way developers and policy actors establish system design dynamics, in which humans assist machines so that they perform their functions. On the other hand, it matters how AI creates political and bureaucratic policy dynamics assisted by AI in policy formulation, implementation, and evaluation. In both situations, these interactions create normative, functional, and symbolic meanings that produce consequences for humans in the policy process and social behavior construction. AI reproduces old policy problems such as ideological bias, reproduction of prejudices and stereotypes, or established organizational dynamics that create implementation problems and design failures. Although AI is a rationalization mechanism for policy processes, it is not a mechanism of perfect rationality. Data sets limit the scope of AI, in addition to design problems in which humans set a goal for the machine. AI is closer to a *machine of muddling through*, in which decisions and tasks continue to be executed in contexts of uncertainty and bounded rationality (Cox, 2019).

When AI is designed to be adopted in the policy process, it incorporates knowledge from various sources to instrumentalize public action, whether augmented or faster. Policy design requires internal dynamics from bureaucrats and policymakers regarding the choice of the mix of instruments and their disposal for coherence and consistency to achieve objectives (Howlett, Mukherjee, & Rayner, 2018; Howlett, 2019; Capano & Howlett, 2020;

Siddiki, 2020). An AI that is applied in public policy involves defining the system's scope, affordances, and characteristics, in which developers, bureaucrats, and policymakers interact to choose algorithm architectures, create databases, train systems, explain these systems, and evaluate their capacity and accuracy to fulfill policy functions, sustaining the system throughout the policy process. In both situations – policy design or system design – biases, stereotypes, values, and worldviews will be fundamental to understanding design choices (Forestal, 2022).

Designing AI means that humans constitute systems to perform a purpose. In many situations, systems design resembles policy design, depending on complex human interactions to choose algorithmic architectures and their instrumental requirements. System design means that AI systems can embody the entire policy design, perform functions as an implementing agent, or embody specific tasks by interacting with humans to solve problems. In this sense, the grounds for interactions between humans and machines is instrumental rationality to create AI systems to augment capacities (Weizenbaum, 1976). In the policy cycle, AI is deployed to augment policy capacities (Filgueiras, 2022b).

In another direction, AI interacts with policymakers and bureaucrats in the policy process (Alon-Barkat & Busuioc, 2023). AI increases policy advice dynamics through recommendation algorithms, selection and hierarchy of preferences, clustering of social groups, and production of prediction and simulation on policy problems and solutions. AI is an instrument that produces organizational rationalization, new ways of thinking, and beliefs about objectives and future policy solutions. It is a pervasive technology driven by society's desire to build a decision system through agents that can control the future and interact with humans differently, defining new modes of social action (Weizenbaum, 1976; Nowotny, 2021). Social action is the essential point of interactions between humans and machines in the policy process: AI transforms how policy actors understand and reason about problems and solutions through opaque technologies that support the entire construction of knowledge in different policy domains.

According to Daugherty and Wilson (2018), the interaction between humans and AI in everyday life unfolds into three dynamics. First, AI *amplifies* analytical capacities and decision-making abilities. Policy decision-makers have bounded rationality because they cannot process all available information and then decide, but AI can look at everything that can be datafied, thereby increasing the human capacity to understand problems and solutions (Simon, 1995). Second, AI makes it possible to *interact* with different audiences. In the policy process, policymakers and bureaucrats can interact with citizens, companies, and other stakeholders more comprehensively (Margetts & John, 2024).

Interfaces amplify collaboration by the mediation of interactions (Campion et al., 2022). Third, AI enables *the embodiment* of a robot that augments a human worker. With their sophisticated sensors, motors, and actuators, AI-enabled machines can recognize people and objects and work safely alongside humans in factories, warehouses, and laboratories. In the public sector, robotics is a future field involving automation and human interactions with robots that perform repetitive or complex tasks (Dunleavy & Margetts, 2024). Amplification, interaction, and embodiment constitute the broader framework for AI in governments, with diverse consequences for performance of public policy and services. This discursive frame creates a technological hype that encourages governments to adopt technology uncritically and without knowledge of its limitations.

Considering these interactive dynamics between AI and policymakers, analysts, and bureaucrats, some questions arise. AI has a totalizing perspective on information, with the expectation of increasing and creating collaborative structures and embodied robots throughout the policy process. This idea is compelling in producing policy change, new modalities of policy learning and advice, new modes of institutionalization and governance, and new perspectives on working with public policy in an augmented way. Although there are many promises about AI in the policy process, doubts should remain about the capacity for practical improvements through technological change or whether new risks are emerging for old problems.

3.4 Risks, Problems, and Catastrophic Ambiguities from Epistocratic Policy

The epistemic changes infused into policy science by AI reinforce policy actors' technocratic thinking (Hartley & Kuecker, 2022). This technocratic thinking derives from convergence defined by data patterns empirically, with greater or lesser receptivity to data and evidence. Technocratic bias is reinforced further when algorithms shape discourses, distribute resources, and increase or reduce people's or groups' visibility. Data and algorithms reproduce self-fulfilling prophecies in many situations through feedback loops, which forge innovative solutions to old policy problems (Mendonça, Filgueiras & Almeida, 2023). In this sense, using AI in the policy process is challenging precisely because it transforms the structure of knowledge, modifying the framing of problems, the knowledge of solutions, and the ways of intervening, governing, and producing changes in society. AI reinforces a governance style based on an epistocratic dynamic, which distrusts democracy as a problem-solving method.

This trend toward a public policy regime based on epistocracy means that the advancement of AI in the government sphere impacts the working of democracy. Epistocracy is "rule by the knowers" rather than "rule by the people" (Estlund, 2008). The hype of AI in governments spreads the idea that it can increase society's trust in the functioning of government institutions, contribute to public integrity, and strengthen accountability (OECD, 2024). By integrating AI into public policy, governments assume a distrust of democracy and its capacity for collective decision-making. AI reinforces epistocracy and creates the conservative imaginary that machines deciding for humans is a better solution (Brennan, 2016).

The epistemic changes spread by AI occur through how it classifies, clusters, hierarchizes, correlates, produces causality, and performs tasks based on data. Following the logic of imitation, AI uses these procedures based on the philosophical premise that humans use these procedures to learn about things, people, and nature and, thus, make decisions and act. The problem is that we do not have complete information about the policy process. Actors' biases shape decision-making. Ideas, values, and opinions shape policy process and sustain decisions and actions on a factual representation of the world rather than precisely on a background rationality (Béland, 2019).

AI in public policy is a tool designed to change the perception and action of policymakers in diverse political contexts. In other words, AI integrated into public policy is a political instrument built from the biases and perspectives of its designers, who introduce affordances that define what is possible for the target audience of a given government intervention in society. Political, social, cultural, and economic biases are extremely important in composing the decision-making process and policy action (Lindblom, 1959; Banuri, Dercon & Gauri, 2019). The fact that AI sustains its decisions on data does not mean that these decisions in the policy process are based on evidence, much less that it is a technical decision. Trial and error, decision-makers' bias, and ideational heuristics are essential to AI design and turn technology into a political artifact. In this way, using AI in the policy process is closer to dynamics based on muddling through, requiring incremental decisions and constant learning (Cox, 2019). Following the trail blazed by Lindblom (1959), integrating AI into public policy does not change the bounded rationality and complexity. Integrating AI into public policy may result in the reproduction of old problems in new knowledge artifacts.

AI, as an epistemic instrument, incorporates – through data – all these biases and conceptions of the world, causing policy advice and learning to occur in a way that discursively and rationally reinforces decision-makers' biases (Eubanks, 2018; Noble, 2018; Mendonça, Filgueiras & Almeida, 2023). This incorporation of biases occurs from data, where bureaucrats and policymakers define algorithmic architectures and databases that will inform the decision-making and carry out tasks automatically. Training and operation databases for AI systems in public policy express – through documents and public records – the choices and decisions of bureaucrats and policymakers, making these systems optimizers of algorithmically institutionalized decision biases (Hong, 2024). AI in public policy requires caution, recognizing the challenges of biased or incomplete datasets and the potential for flawed models to generate misleading policy outcomes.

This dynamic design and use of AI creates a series of risks in the policy process. There are risks related to algorithmic injustice, organizational risks, and the possibility of rogue AI. Algorithmic unfairness arises from AI systems' algorithmically institutionalized biases, relating to issues of gender, race, ethnicity, sexuality, and social groups. When algorithms reproduce racial bias, for instance, a person can see how certain conceptions of the world are assimilated in technical ways (Noble, 2018; Buolamwini, 2023). In many situations, AI algorithms reproduce biases or discrimination from a lack of diversity in the technological design process (Benjamin, 2019; Hong, 2024). As a result, sexism, racism, and other forms of discrimination are built into the machine learning algorithms that underlie the technology behind many "intelligent" systems that shape how we are characterized and advertised.

In many instances, such discrimination stems from a computer industry comprised of few women, black people, or people of different sexual orientations, for example (Crawford, 2021). This issue of inclusion in the design of technologies applied in public policy is fundamental to avoid bias and ensure co-creation and transparency processes that enable correct application (Noble, 2018; Yuwono et al., 2024). On the other hand, algorithmic injustice arises from data and the low visibility that data gives to topics related to social justice. Data incorporates society's biases, and the extent to which it makes certain social groups visible or invisible is fundamental to AI's performance in the policy process (Gitelman, 2013). Public policy formulated and implemented with AI has the potential to create or reinforce inequalities. Algorithmic injustice requires that the design of AI applied to public policy introduce important innovations, such as inclusive co-creation of systems and algorithmic impact assessment focusing on inequalities in the policy process.

Organizational risks refer to the possibility of systems malfunctioning because of organizational failures. Simple bugs in an AI's reward function could cause it to misbehave. For example, OpenAI researchers accidentally modified a language model to produce "maximally bad output." Gain-of-function research – where researchers intentionally train a harmful AI to assess its risks – could expand the frontier of dangerous AI capabilities and create new organizational hazards. For example, in the pharmaceutical field, AI has a dual potential to discover drugs, depending on how human control and regulation are steered toward human well-being (Urbina et al., 2022). Public organizations such as the Federal Court of Accounts in Brazil use a ChatGPT-based instrument to optimize processes and perform repetitive tasks. Organizational failures and the absence of measures to control risks and avoid human errors produce catastrophic results for organizations. Public policy requires public organizations to build security measures and address organizational dynamics such as segregation of duties, internal controls, and systems security measures so that operations and policy tasks are unaffected. From a risk perspective, organizations demand actions in line with the principles of trustworthy AI and taking accountability to mitigate the risks (Curtis, Gillespie & Lockey, 2023).

Finally, we have the risks of rogue AI. Rogue AIs are dangerous and powerful AIs that would execute harmful goals, irrespective of whether the outcomes are intended by humans (Bengio, 2023). Rogue AIs imply an idea of intentionally using powerful AI to produce social harm. The assumption is that there is a misalignment between the use of technology and the purposes for which it was designed. For example, there is the possibility of using deepfakes created with AI to influence elections on social media (Diakopoulos & Johnson, 2021), explore markets (Lin, 2017), or generate political polarization (Jacobs, 2024). Likewise, AI enables lethal autonomous weapons that identify human targets to eliminate them (Russell, 2022) or to create bioweapons (Urbina et al., 2022). AI threatens humanity with catastrophic or even existential consequences in these situations.

AI is not a neutral instrument or an absolute technique in these risk situations. Humans designed and deployed it in diverse policy domains to accomplish diverse objectives based on data-driven knowledge. In this sense, AI is an ambiguous, dual, and opaque technology in the policy process, with diverse consequences for society. Conceived as a policy instrument, the possibility of optimizing the policy cycle is great in the sense of increasing information and the possibilities of organizational rationalization of governments, and augment policy capacity to achieve political objectives. The ambiguity lies in the fact that the design of AI systems can take on different facets and nurture the fantasies and beliefs of policymakers and bureaucrats (Filgueiras, 2022b), and in the same way, produce ambiguous results for society. Applying AI in the public policy cycle means taking risks and new possibilities to increase policy capacities.

4 Modeling a Disruptive Policy Cycle with AI

The technical discussion presented in the previous section is important for understanding the framework of AI integration in the policy process. In Section 2, we analyzed how AI challenges the construction of knowledge in public policy. In Section 3, we discussed AI as a policy instrument and how technology affords policy action. In Section 4, we will explore the impact of AI on policy work. First, how policy design and system design meet and imply new capacities for policymakers. Second, how the integration of AI in the policy process implies specific dynamics of instrument constituencies. Finally, in this section, we discuss how AI fits into policy advice.

The traditional view of policy sciences understands the policy cycle as a central element for understanding the dynamics through which a policy is formed and implemented with outcomes for society. The public policy cycle is an analytical device for explaining and prescribing a policy (Howlett & Ramesh, 2003). Fundamentally, the policy cycle is layers that follow one another, but not in an orderly or sequential manner. The literature considers the policy cycle a heuristic resource formed by identifying the policy problem, formulation, decision-making, implementation, and evaluation.

As we detail later in the section, the introduction of AI adds new dimensions across the policy cycle. However, in the traditional view throughout the policy cycle a flow of information converts into decision and implementation processes. In a problem definition, for example, agenda-setting issues involve knowing the problems and, based on this knowledge, deciding and acting in the formulation processes (Cháques-Bonafont, Palau & Baumgartner, 2015). In implementation, for instance, information is central for governments to conduct their interventions and establish knowledge about the relationships between organizations and citizens to achieve effective outcomes that produce social change (Peeters, Pressman & Wildavsky, 1984; Rentería & Cejudo, 2023). Information plays a significant role in the policy cycle and enables constituting the cycle as a broader policy system and its effects on governments' practical action (Howlett & Ramesh, 2003; Baumgartner & Jones, 2015).

The policy cycle strengthens a perspective that supports policy work from policy analysis. Understanding the policy cycle provides a broader framework of policy science as an interdisciplinary, analytical, and practical work (De Leon, 1981). At the heart of policy science is analysis and how it informs policy practice. From the policy analysis perspective, information is central to advising government action. Then public policy is an epistemic action that relies on information to shape different decisions. Public policy manuals define different steps by which a policy is formulated and implemented. For example, Bardach

(2012) defines the policy analysis practice as an agency that defines the problem, assembles evidence, constructs alternatives, selects criteria, designs outcomes, confronts trade-offs, decides, and tells a story. Information and various micro or macro decisions are central to these actions and define the practical dynamics surrounding government activities.

Throughout the policy cycle's dynamics, information and advice are central and shape practical action (Wilson, 2009). The knowledge and recommendations that emerge in public policy are humanly created and involve interests, opinions, and perspectives on problems and solutions (Lowi, 1964). Because it is based on interests, opinions, and perspectives, public policy involves complex interactions between actors based on exchanging information and meanings for government action. In many situations, as Bardach states, "[t]he problem-solving process – being a process of trial and error – is iterative, so you usually must repeat each of these steps, sometimes more than once" (Bardach, 2012, p. xvii).

The policy cycle is an analytical device, and places at its center the idea that a public policy's success depends on analytical capacities. Analytical capacities, in turn, depend on the central idea of policy analysis, which is the method for structuring information and providing opportunities to define alternatives for policymakers. Analytical capacities involve individual, organizational, and systemic approaches (Wu, Ramesh & Howlett, 2015). Individual capacities involve technical skills and knowledge about the substance of policy. Organizational capacities concern the budget and human resources for organizations to accumulate and disseminate knowledge. Finally, systemic capacities concern high-quality educational and training institutions and opportunities for knowledge generation, mobilization, and use (Howlett, 2015). Considering this idea of capacities and the role of information in the policy cycle, we can state that all public policy activities depend on knowledge and recommendations (Wilson, 2009).

Policy analysis depends on the capacities to frame solutions, create action situations, and define scripts for action (Ostrom, 2005). AI disrupts this perspective on policy analysis. AI changes the entire dynamics of policy analysis, and it changes regarding information flows and knowledge production. There are two reasons why AI disrupts the policy cycle. AI increases the speed of analysis and dissemination of information (Valle-Cruz et al., 2020) and augments analytical capacities in the individual, organizational, and systemic dimensions (Veale & Brass, 2019).

In agenda setting, for instance, problem identification combines existing administrative data with more granular or dynamic data collected in social media, platforms, or distributed systems for decision-making. AI enables policy analysts to shape unstructured and unconventional data through text mining and NLP (Allahyari et al. 2017). Furthermore, the possibility of using large language models for policy analysis is disruptive and fast to produce intelligence and advice (Safaei & Longo, 2024, Logan, 2024). In policy formulation, AI could provide some simulations about policy to assess viability. It could also help to improve prior decisions with machine learning algorithms and to expand or intertwine government decisions within multiple governmental layers (Valle-Cruz & Sandoval-Almanzán, 2022). In policy implementation, AI enables organizational rationalization and optimization and increases the organizational capacity to produce effective deliveries for society and connect citizens and governments via public service. Associated with the use of robotics, AI makes it possible to increase capacities and delivery speed in a more holistic way for the State and public administration (Dunleavy & Margetts, 2024).

The possibility of new tools throughout the policy cycle has provided a new paradigm for policy analysis and new work practices in policy formulation and implementation. With augmented and faster information, the actions of policy actors change because of changes in how policy is developed with data. Big data and incorporating AI systems into the policy cycle modify procedural and substantive instruments, in turn altering policymakers' and bureaucrats' actions in the policy process (Giest, 2017). From the perspective of policy instruments, AI can be a regulatory instrument, automating activities related to the use of government authority (Yeung, 2018). Likewise, AI can be a nodal instrument, modifying the relationship between citizens and government (Margetts & Dorobantu, 2019). AI can also shape fiscal management of the budget and public resources, being a treasury instrument (Valle Cruz, Fernandez-Cortez & Gil-Garcia, 2022). Finally, AI is an entire organizational instrument, changing public service's institutional framework (Dunleavy & Margetts, 2024).

Introducing AI in the policy cycle disrupts how policies are formulated and implemented. Policy science has a new layer of complexity for policy analysis and work. Over the public policy cycle, based on human interactive processes, there is an AI system modeling work based on interactions between humans and machines (Janssen & Helbig, 2018). For each phase of public policy cycle, AI systems modeling is used to change the policy production chain. The disruptive element is AI creating and accelerating knowledge about policy cycle elements, with humans and machines interacting to create solutions, set up and review government action, or predict and simulate outcomes and impacts. A new layer of policy work is to model databases and AI systems that will produce optimization across decision-making and task execution in the different policy cycle phases, innovating all activities related to analytical capacities and administrative execution.

Policies for electrical power transmission in the United States are an example of this dynamic. Power flow is a cornerstone of electrical power system operations. Failures in the power flow compromise the entire electrical distribution system, negatively impacting the functioning of a country's industry and commerce. Energy policy represents an important topic, and complex systems based on machine learning have gradually supported its implementation. The availability of massive historical and synthesized data and the repeated need to solve related problems make machine learning an omnipresent technology to approach the challenges of power transmission. AI can be especially helpful in optimal power flow (OPF) analysis – evaluating the most efficient and reliable flow of electricity through a transmission network (Hentenryck, 2021). The United States has made massive investments in data modeling and electrical power transmission flow analysis to advance optimization and energy policy aimed at environmental issues.

AI integrated into energy policy presents some challenges related to modeling data from diverse users of the electricity system. Problems in data modeling can harm populations not identified or categorized in the dataset, leading to exclusion. AI can lead to biased outcomes when training data does not accurately represent real-world conditions. In the case of energy policy, rural populations may be underrepresented in the dataset, leading to technological redlines. An AI model trained on power system data without adequate information on poor communities could recommend infrastructure investments that fail to adequately serve those communities.

The idea of simulating and predicting a policy is not exactly a new field of knowledge in policy process. Policy modeling is an important field of knowledge in public policy, working with predictions and simulations to guide the formulation. Policy modeling is an academic or empirical research work, that is supported using different theories as well as quantitative or qualitative models and techniques, to analytically evaluate the past (causes) and future (effects) of any policy on society, anywhere and anytime (Estrada, 2011). Policy modeling is related to the policy simulation through computational techniques and calculations. However, it does not support the idea of AI. As we said before, AI assumes that humans and machines interact to achieve a purpose. The concept of policy modeling does not require this interactive dynamic. With AI focusing on how decision makers, bureaucrats, and citizens interact with machines, modeling extends to modeling policy work, in which predictions and simulations are generated by modeling AI systems to produce public decisions and task execution, repeatedly and driven by feedback.

In a particular public policy, each element of the policy cycle is superimposed on an element of the modeling policy work. We understand the modeling policy work as the entire cycle of analytical actions necessary and sufficient for humans to model a public policy by designing and deploying AI-based systems. The activity of modeling AI-based systems overrides policy work. AI makes decisions and performs tasks necessary to understand public problems, formulate alternatives, implement organizational actions, and evaluate outcomes and impacts. Beyond policy work, applying AI throughout the policy process initiates a new work based on modeling AI systems that will perform different purposes in a singular public policy. Innovations with AI applied to public policy mean a different way of performing policy analysis and implying the knowledge generated throughout the policy cycle. Imagining a future government where its public policies are formulated and implemented with AI, the disruption in policy design lies in the fact that it incorporates a system design layer, which has its own dilemmas and problems.

The modeling policy work is the sociotechnical reengineering of the public policy cycle through human interactions (a traditional policy cycle) and human-machine interactions (disruptive policy). The modeling policy work is part of a broader concept of sociotechnical reengineering inscribed in the use of digital technologies (Frischmann & Selinger, 2018; Filgueiras, 2022b) and reinstitutionalizing politics and society through algorithms (Mendonça, Filgueiras & Almeida, 2023). The modeling policy work means that human-machine interactions shift the policy dynamics in two ways: first, the human activities to design AI systems to sustain a policy; second, how humans and machines interact, and actors' agency shifts by new dynamics of policy advice. Table 1 compares the elements of traditional and modeling policy work.

Incorporating AI into the policy cycle does not mean reducing its importance as an analytical device. It continues to exist but with an overlapping layer, because the entire policy process is traversed by the modeling cycle. AI's effects on the policy cycle arise from the fact that humans and machines interact in the dimensions of system design and in the dimension of application. In other words, on one hand, there is the constitution of AI as an instrument or mix of instruments applied throughout the policy cycle. Designing AI in the public policy cycle follows an instrument constituency dynamic, involving actors to design and deploy systems applied throughout decision-making and task execution. On the other hand, AI changes the nature of policy advice. AI systems, especially those based on prediction and simulation, as well as recommendation systems, change the logic of policy advice, shaping policymakers' and bureaucrats' actions throughout the policy cycle.

The result of incorporating AI into the policy cycle is the disruption of policymaking. This disruption shapes distinctive styles of policy governance. Traditional policy work comprises different styles, which can be based on state

Table 1 Traditional and modeling work in policy analysis.

Elements	Traditional policy work	Modeling policy work
Instrument constituency	Interested in the choices of different actors for the instrument and its retention	Modeling of data and abstract system elements
Policy advice	Knowledge of the problems and recommendations that emerge from consultancies, actors, lobbying, and parties or civil society	Modeling recommendation, simulation, and predictive systems
Policy dynamics	Human interactions	Human-machine interactions
Governance styles	Democratic	Epistocratic

Source: own elaboration.

command-and-control or the composition of policy networks and more horizontal modes involving civil society, nonprofit organizations, markets, and social groups (Stoker, 1998; Salamon, 2002; Klijn & Koppenjan, 2012; Sorensen & Torfing, 2005; Peters & Pierre, 2016). All these governance styles share the idea that a democratic regime is essential in composing public policies. Here, when we discuss adding modeling policy work, we mean transforming policy governance, including another style based on technical knowledge. Adding a layer of modeling policy work governs the policy cycle with an epistocratic dynamic. Epistocracy is the idea that good political decisions should be based on knowledge rather than an aggregation of opinions (Estlund, 2008). The epistocratic style stems from the idea that democracies are incapable of delivering good solutions and advocates epistocratic procedures to protect political communities from the rule of ignorance. Technical solutions would overcome political disputes, thus enabling a more efficient government (Brennan, 2016). This epistocratic style resonates with the idea that public policy based on AI systems is neutral and instruments are designed technically.

Incorporating AI into the policy cycle adds a layer to traditional policy work through systems modeling. In the problem definition, traditional policy work involves using opinion polls, monitoring media, identifying issues in social groups (Baumgartner & Jones, 2015), gathering the national mood, or gathering ideas from visible and invisible actors (Kingdon, 1995). By introducing AI for problem identification, governments can collect data from multiple sources, including social media, automated media monitoring, and data and evidence collected during implementation processes. For instance, text mining techniques and using LLMs provide rapid ways of building agendas (Gyódi et al., 2023). Collecting data to identify policy problems requires new policy work driven by database modeling, data governance, and skills to feed AI systems.

At the formulation stage, interactions between actors are fundamental in constructing policy alternatives, involving visible and invisible actors who interact to formulate a policy (Kingdom, 1995), usually through trial and error and incremental decisions (Lindblom, 1959). Introducing AI in the formulation stage shifts the dynamics of defining alternatives, providing means to simulate and predict results reliably (Ramezani, 2023). In both dimensions, decisions are shaped with information constructed in diverse ways. In traditional policy work, information emanates from actors, studies, benchmarks, and interests. In the modeling policy cycle, information emanates from technical work with data and the construction of systems.

This technical work involves the conceptualization and design dynamics of systems, in which human agents define systems' scope and purpose. Considering problem identification and policy formulation, decision-making contrasts two distinct decision dynamics. While traditional policy work demands information exchange, conflicts, or consensus among actors, modeling policy work depends on purely technical decisions such as building data warehouses, training databases, or designing systems (Coeckelbergh & Saetra, 2023). Policies can be formulated through real-time communication with citizens and businesses, modifying the formulation in real-time with machine learning (Margetts & John, 2024). In policymaking situations, AI integration changes the conditions of agenda-setting, whether through direct communication with citizens or businesses or by collecting data from social media platforms (Giest, 2017). AI is disruptive in policymaking because it changes the frames and affordances of political communication, transforming how policymakers can understand public problems.

Implementation links government purpose and the world of actions and outcomes. Implementation is a function of government decision, government management and oversight, and resulting execution by bureaucracy (Hill & Hupe, 2009). In implementation, the traditional dynamic implies the existence of organizational structures that provide the action necessary to achieve outcomes. In organizational structures, the choice of institutional architecture is essential to shaping bureaucrats' and society's actions (Olsen, 2006). Furthermore, it involves incorporating organizations from the private and nonprofit sectors. The core implementation challenge is governance and crafting implementation structures that deliver services for society (Imperial, 2021).

The choice of institutional architecture implies top-down implementation structures following hierarchical guidelines or bottom-up models, which start with society and networks to policy implementation. Top-down models frame implementation in command-and-control relationships, where implementation is the ability to achieve predicted consequences after initial conditions have been met, such as legislation and funds (Pressman & Wildavsky, 1984). Bottom-up structures, on the other hand, identify the actors' network involved in service delivery and incorporate their goals and strategies as part of the policy-making process (Hjern & Porter, 1981). Bottom-up models recognize the importance of street-level bureaucrats and the discretionary nature of their actions, where small decisions can change the course of policy implementation (Lipsky, 2010). Implementation by bottom-up structures is based on the idea of policy effectiveness and how they depend on decentralized authority relationships based on formal and informal institutions, such as expertise, skill, and proximity to essential tasks that an organization performs (Elmore, 1979).

Modeling policy work understands that implementation implies the existence of AI systems that operate as mechanisms for rationalizing organizations implementing policy. This dynamic means that AI's deployment in policy implementation institutionalizes services through digital platforms that modify discretionary relationships with citizens. The discretion of government action is transferred to platforms with AI systems that perform organizational tasks and make decisions that directly affect citizens' lives (Mendonça, Filgueiras & Almeida, 2023). In modeling policy work, the work of policymakers is not defined by authority relationships within bureaucracies or policy networks or with citizens. The choice of algorithmic architectures, validation, and verification processes, creating experiments and prototypes, and the scaling of service provision to humans – in this case citizens – interacting with machines defines the innovative policy work. Policymakers choose the AI affordances applied in an automation of policy. These choices imply creating services implemented through AI systems that provide automation, speed, accuracy, and a low possibility of deviations (Veale & Brass, 2019; Valle-Cruz et al., 2020).

Implementation through AI reinforces the technocratic character of digital governments. The implementation process is now shaped by computer systems that collect data and provide services digitally. However, implementation through AI and platforms implies that policy decision-makers, data analysts, and developers interact to construct information, facilitate framing, define action situations, and adjust action scripts to political preferences. In other words, data analysts and developers act in predefined policy contexts and are essential to defining the political frameworks for government action (Van der Voort et al., 2019).

Finally, policy evaluation in traditional policy work is conducted with monitoring structures and data that allow the assessment of outcomes, effectiveness, and impact of policies and programs on society (Vedung, 2009). The goal of evaluations is to generate knowledge and recommendations for policymakers and bureaucrats to review action or reinforce instruments to achieve policy objectives (Weiss, 1998). Although there are political and institutional constraints for evaluation (Bovens, t'Hart & Kuipers, 2008), policymakers and bureaucrats use knowledge generated by evaluations to establish value on the policies implemented and learn about corrections. Evaluation is crafted for different uses and depends on analytical capacities developed within organizations (Pattyn & Brans, 2015). AI's use in evaluation makes it possible to create real-time monitoring structures and to automate evaluations depending on the quality of data generated. AI can automate evaluations with text mining and consistently analyze policy outcomes, effectiveness, and impact (Sun & Medaglia, 2019). In modeling policy work, the choice of algorithmic architectures and coding and data structuring work is critical for consistently delivering evaluation automation. As with implementation, policymakers, data analysts, and developers interact and define the policy uses and affordances of AI-powered evaluation.

For example, in China, during the COVID-19 pandemic, AI was developed to evaluate, in real-time, nonpharmacological approaches to pandemic control due to its restriction on people's liberty and economic impacts. The system includes three components: (1) a general simulation framework that models different policies to comparable network-flow control problems; (2) a reinforcement learning (RL) oracle to explore the upper-bound execution results of policies; and (3) comprehensive protocols for converting the RL results to policy-assessment measures, including execution complexity, effectiveness, cost and benefit, and risk. The system evaluated three approaches using data from Beijing: city lockdown, community quarantine, and route management. This system aimed to assess and perceive the environment of COVID-19 infection and evaluate which course of action to take given the perceived environment. This case was a successful AI development for real-time assessment, with practical implications for reviewing policies to combat a COVID-19 pandemic situation. This tool sustains policymakers in reviewing and simulating situations of deepening or relaxing nonpharmacological policy to combat COVID-19 in China (Song et al., 2022).

In disruptive public policy, traditional policy work iterates with modeling work for data and AI systems throughout the policy cycle. The disruptive element is how policymaking depends on active interactions between bureaucrats, policymakers, and system developers. Conversely, citizens interact passively with interfaces – platforms – that have embedded AI making decisions and performing tasks. Developers become central actors in public policy designed in the context of digital governments. This dynamic provides essential institutional changes in the way public policy becomes path-dependent on data, creates algorithmic regulation, and transforms procedural and substantive instruments to achieve objectives discursively framed (Mendonça, Filgueiras & Almeida, 2023). In this framework, different ethical problems and varied risks might occur, for which no adequate governance exists. Using AI systems in public policy, although they have the potential to expand evidence and knowledge, is dependent on political frames offered in the system design dimension (Van der Voort et al., 2019; Newman & Mintron, 2023).

In the policy cycle, AI produces epistemic changes directly affecting public policy work. Human-machine interactions, in this context, are essential to the policy context. Epistemic changes require new capacities from policymakers and bureaucrats due to the interactions between traditional and modeling policy work. The disruptive point is that policymakers and bureaucrats must consider computational modeling a new skill for public policy. Policy cycle and computational modeling interact in a complex way, producing substantial changes in policy analysis and public policy practice (Süsser et al., 2021). This circumstance – where modeling and traditional policy work interact – has implications for policy science in terms of knowledge production and action, supporting new dynamics within the policy process.

In the development of AI in public policy, there are new dynamics on the horizon for policymakers, creating new challenges that span the entire policy cycle. Integrating AI into the policy cycle implies a new mode of action shaped by interactions between humans and machines. AI does not represent autonomous agents, but its use in policy has implications for government agencies. The following section will analyze how AI is created by actors and in what political context.

4.1 Instrument Constituency and AI System Design

The debate over whether AI is an instrument or agent is substantial in the field of computer science. In terms of public policy, the definition of AI is as an epistemic instrument (Alvarado, 2023) that transforms the way policymakers, decision-makers, bureaucrats, and networks make decisions and act based on knowledge generated with data. As a central epistemic instrument in the policy cycle, its constitution and design are essential. In the dynamics of interactions between humans and machines, modeling policy work implies a dynamic design of systems that will constitute actions so that AI can influence problem identification, formulation, decision-making, implementation, and evaluation. More specifically, in human-machine interactions, we address the way in which humans constitute AI-based instruments (Daugherty & Wilson, 2018).

Understanding how different agents act to create AI in public policy can be understood better in the dynamics of instrument constituencies. Instrument constituencies are networks of diverse types of institutions and organizations that share a common interest in promoting a specific policy instrument and related practices for their own benefit in material terms or sharing ideas (Voß & Simons, 2014; Simons & Voß, 2018). In general, instrument constituencies connect networks of scientists, design experts, consultants, public administrators, and technicians who design and deploy instruments in policy process. This actors' network has an interest in developing, retaining, and expanding the instrument, and they work to institutionalize it in policy practice. In the instrument constituencies approach, we can see how to design AI to integrate it into the policy process. Political choices are at the heart of AI design.

In the case of AI conceived as an instrument, constituencies are formed by networks of the aforementioned actors plus developers in private companies that control the global communications infrastructure – big techs. Big techs are in the political stream, promoting AI as a solution to various social, economic, political, cultural, and environmental problems (Ulnicane & Aden, 2023; Khanal, Zhang & Taeihagh, 2025). Big techs are essential in the dynamics of instrument constituency because they approach a techno-solutionist perspective for different problems. Instrument constituencies act as a network in a policy context defined by the digital transformation package, with the potential to change all types of policy instruments (Margetts & Dorobantu, 2019; Yeung, 2018; Dunleavy & Margetts, 2024). In this policy context, public policy has its instrumental dynamics modified by the system design applied to automate and rationalize public organizations.

Constituting AI-based policy instruments is not a neutral activity, much less a technically constructed one (Russell, 2019; Xavier, 2025). The AI instrument constituency involves networks of scientists, policymakers, bureaucrats, industry, design experts, consultants, and software developers who interact politically. These actors dedicate themselves to articulating and promoting solutions regardless of the problem context, with the aim of producing technologies. This network provides the encounter between the solution and the problem, mobilizing articulations around solutions in search of problems (Béland & Howlett, 2016). The legitimization of this process occurs within a context of functional evaluation of the instruments, extending their application in society. Moreover, this framework relies on the nature of the problems and how epistemic lenses underlie institutional and social relations, as well as the role the instruments can play within such structures (Lascoumes & Lé Galès, 2007).

Instrument constituencies deploy AI as a pervasive instrument across the policy cycle and change all policy instruments – nodality, authority, treasury, and organization. Instrument constituencies change the configuration of government, being a point of deep hype about AI's potentials and challenges, and the visible and invisible interests that permeate political articulations. The design of technologies applied in governments is politically motivated, given the economic interests in retaining technological instruments (Mendonça, Filgueiras & Almeida, 2023). The legitimacy of these instruments is based on an order of efficiency as AI increases and amplifies the productivity of the public sector (Dunleavy & Margetts, 2024). Discourses on the efficiency of AI policies abound, but evidence from productive sectors suggests that productivity gains are modest, with AI primarily serving to automate repetitive activities (Acemoglu, 2024). The point we argue in this Element is that AI does not necessarily amplify productivity but transforms the epistemic bases of policy instruments.

Although an epistocratic style of governance emerges from AI, this does not mean it is a neutral and effective instrument. Its constitution is permeated by economic interests that shape the perspective from which the government will adopt AI. For example, leading companies in AI development, such as NVidia, Amazon, Microsoft, SpaceX, and Meta, are major solutions suppliers to the US government and other governments worldwide. Currently, these companies engage in deep political debates with specific ideological perspectives according to the economic interests of a given situation. Since they control the global communication infrastructure, their power is strongly constitutive of the framing of technological solutions applied in governments (Rikap, 2021). The intersection of these instrument constituencies with the government organizes the AI hype and the framings of the policy objectives that AIs intend to achieve when integrated into public policy. In other words, big techs influence policy content because they integrate into political, policy, and problem streams and forge windows of opportunity to create policies (Khanal, Zhang & Taeihagh, 2025).

Instrument constituencies involve design AI systems from policy modeling, defining systems' abstract objectives, conceptualizing and choosing algorithmic architectures, modeling databases, defining techniques, and coding and assessing accuracy, as well as validating systems for making decisions and carrying out policy tasks.

AI instruments have political implications as machine learning algorithms mean "a way of gathering and ordering society's knowledge that fundamentally transforms how the state and society come to understand each other" (Amoore, 2022, p. 21). Furthermore, AI instrument constituencies act by monopolizing knowledge and turning data and information into commodified resources (Rikap, 2021). As a result, we have programmable and codified institutions that change policymakers' behavior in a broader context (Mendonça, Filgueiras & Almeida, 2023). According to Louise Amoore (2014), working with AI requires a different type of ability from designers who are more imaginative and intuitive, applied to governing society innovatively. AI instrument constituencies act by defining the steering of public policy, embedding all the policy cycle in systems that perform policy interventions and impact society.

In other words, AI-based sociotechnical systems are produced on an industrial scale and constructed on algorithms embedded in data processing platforms, shared or marketed in the cloud, with ready-made architectures that are customizable for different problems, in both public and private sectors. Scientists and developers promote the choice of algorithmic architectures based on trial and error concerning the problem, choosing the solution that presents the best accuracy and optimization (Amoore, 2022). The design dynamics of AI systems, in many ways, emulate the dynamics of policy design: elements of rationalization and optimization are sought to implement a politically shaped idea. AI instruments are politically constructed and guided by interests, perspectives, and opinions like policy instruments. The idea of austerity in economic crises infuses a digital transformation perspective (Mendonça, Filgueiras & Almeida, 2023). Furthermore, austerity makes governments dependent on private cloud-based data infrastructures that give big techs an intellectual monopoly on political ideas (Rikap, 2021).

An example of this process is how, in a context of strong conservative opposition to immigration policies, the use of AI to control borders has grown aggressively. This example of AI use is for them to classify, divide, and demarcate boundaries in data. These AIs use deep learning techniques that involve much more than the deployment of technologies at the border. These AIs are reordering what the border means and how to imagine the boundaries of the political community (Amoore, 2024).

Machine learning algorithms are solutions looking for problems within broader organizational processes (Filgueiras, 2022b). Although there are technical measurements of an algorithm's accuracy, it does not allow checking the degree of adherence, coherence, and consistency when applied in the policy process. The technical accuracy of algorithms does not consider policy objectives, public values, justice criteria, or the solution's effectiveness because systems designers consider the accuracy of knowledge, not its epistemological status, aroused in confronting reality. AI-based policy modeling means that the network of instrument constituencies interacts politically with a view to achieving a goal. Industry, developers, and scientists benefit materially from the industrial development of AI, defining actions aimed at the permanence and retention of AI-based instruments and their use in public policy.

The permanence and retention of AI-based policy instruments mean a struggle to adapt systems to policy contexts infused with broader political and institutional orientations based on interests and values. Ideas, therefore, count in the broader framework of technology design (Mendonça, Filgueiras & Almeida, 2023). Thus, AI design is a political struggle to realize an idea framed in discursively expressed political interests of instrumental constituencies. In this case, AI design in public policy fits into techno-solutionism (Paul, 2022; Sætra, 2023). Techno-solutionism is the metaphysical power of advanced technology to transmute the universe's complex, indeterminate nature into obedient, mechanical certainty to be manipulated by the fantasies and fads of policymakers. The AI hype in public policy stems from techno-solutionist ideas that enable constituents to retain policy instruments (Khanal, Zhang & Taeihagh, 2025).

For example, the digital welfare state is based on the premise of redesigning all welfare policies through digital instruments. Machine learning algorithms can perform different tasks related to the welfare state, promoting greater access for society (Coles-Kemp et al., 2020). However, they often are developed in line with a logic of control and dispositions around surveillance and efficiency that challenge careful engagements (Zakharova, Jarke & Kaun, 2024). For example, the Danish government built a surveillance behemoth, dedicated to increasing surveillance against citizens receiving welfare state benefits (Kayser-Bril, 2020). In the case of Danish reforms between 2002 and 2019, the public sector transferred responsibility for key infrastructure to private actors through digitalization. As Collington (2021) points out, the main objective of public sector digitalization has been the growth of Denmark's nascent digital technology industries as part of the state's wider export-led growth strategy, adopted in response to functional pressures on the welfare state model. Fiscal stability drives the reforms in Denmark and has produced a retrenchment of critical assets and capacities (Collington, 2021).

Instrument constituencies therefore are central to defining the frames of AI applied in public policy. The networks of actors participating in the instrument constituency strive to realize ideas that create the frames from which AI technologies will be deployed to realize policy ideas. The network of instrument constituencies strives to define the objectives, data modeling, choice of algorithmic architectures, coding, and framing of system outcomes, to compose all or part of the policy design through AI. Incorporating AI into policy design happens by trial and error, so that the policy analysis that results from using AI confirms and disseminates the results expected by constituents and their partners in an opaque and unaccountable manner. In many situations, AI applied to public policy confirms policymakers' bias in a network of business and control of central infrastructures to develop opaque and unaccountable technologies (Alon-Barkat and Busuoic, 2023).

4.2 Policy Advice in the AI Era

Policy advice is the other side of the AI coin when applied to public policy. In the instrument constituency dynamic, we deal with how public policy actors and industry interact to build and feed AI systems. On the policy advice side, we consider how policy actors receive AI outputs and recommendations like advice to act in policy practice. Policy advice is the set of activities that support policymakers' decisions by analyzing problems and connecting them with solutions and recommendations (Hallingan, 1995). Policy advice activities start from problems and define courses of action for decision-makers (Althaus, 2013). Policy advice encompasses the epistemic nature of policy science and applies to the entire policy cycle (Wilson, 2009). Thus, policy advice is a special type of policy work that connects problems and solutions. Furthermore, policy advice is a complex system that provides decision-makers with a political perspective through values and beliefs, on the one hand, and knowledge through evidence and information (Veselý, 2017). Disruption in public policy arises from the fact that AI provides policy advice, both in a macro dimension of policy overall, and in a micro dimension, which involves small decisions and tasks.

Sharing information, knowledge about problems, and policy recommendations for action is the heart of policy advice. Typically, multiple actors and multiple levels provide policy advice. Actors provide information, knowledge, and recommendations for action to policymakers. These actors include both individuals and organizations. Among multiple actors, policy advice encompasses the actions of consultants, academics, scientists, third-sector organizations, philanthropic organizations, or international organizations. There are levels of policy advice that include the influence of the knowledge generated on policymakers' and bureaucrats' action, on the one hand, and the broader organizational action of the government (Veselý, 2017). Furthermore, policy advice relates more directly to policy capacities, especially those related to analytical capacities (Craft, Head & Howlett, 2024).

The practice of policy advice is fundamental in constructing knowledge and in converting it into policy action, both at the individual and organizational levels (Wilson, 2009; Craft, Head & Howlett, 2024). Policy advice builds knowledge through the analysis of outcomes, production of evidence, use of data in business intelligence, studies focused on a policy topic, or recommendations that emanate from experts and scientists in a given field of knowledge. Recommendations, therefore, are central to policy advice and they connect problems with changes in policy work (Veselý, 2017). Modeling AI systems for the entire public policy cycle transforms the dynamics of policy advice. The heart of AI's use is to transform the entire epistemic basis of public policy through systems that perform predictions and simulations quickly and reliably. Using recommendation algorithms is fundamental to generate and disseminate content and change policy actors' course of action. Algorithmic recommenders are systems aimed at generating meaningful recommendations for content or products that might interest a given set of users. Algorithmic recommendation systems' main function is to estimate a utility function that automatically and mathematically predicts, ranks, and presents the user's top preferences for a specific content or product (Schrage, 2020).

Government platforms embed recommendation algorithms and produce content for policy analysts. Another alternative is to create LLM that uses different techniques that enable the generation of knowledge and influence on action. For example, the Federal Court of Accounts (TCU) in Brazil developed ChatTCU, a chatbot based on the use of GPT-4 and the retrieval-augmented generation (RAG) technique to integrate all the specialized knowledge produced by auditors and system users in Brazil that recommends or generates audit and policy evaluation content. This content recommendation standardizes knowledge among auditors and represents a radical change in auditing and monitoring public policies implemented by the Brazilian federal government (Silva et al., 2024). AI's use adds a new interactive dynamic of knowledge production and infusion of action. Policy advice dynamics go beyond human interactions and incorporate relationships between humans and machines to shape policy content. The example of ChatTCU in Brazil means that knowledge emanating from public policy monitoring and accountability processes disseminates a new type of public action driven by interaction with chatbots.

LLM's usage has the potential to produce automatic policy advisers, increasing science's capacity to support the practice of public policy. AI has the potential to produce evidence syntheses in all fields of knowledge, such as medicine and health (Nowak, 2022), environment (Wani et al., 2024), and education (Ifenthaler et al., 2024). AI has interacted with scientists and experts and changed how science operates, creating difficulties and disruption in the construction of knowledge. Large language models and other AI systems could be excellent at synthesizing scientific evidence for policymakers. However, this use requires appropriate safeguards and humans in the loop (Tyler et al., 2023; Dwivedi et al., 2023).

AI's use shifts the logic of policy advice, increasing and accelerating knowledge and modifying the practice of policy work. AI transforms knowledge construction, transforming, in turn, individual actions, organizational frameworks, and institutional dynamics. AI will not replace policymakers, but it can enable a comprehensive, faster, and more efficient approach to policymaking in the short run and potentially offer policymakers different options. The premise is that in the dynamics of the policy process, humans and machines will interact to generate new forms of policy advice for recommending and shaping government action. Assuming the inherent risks, policymakers, bureaucrats, lobbyists, consultants, members of civil society organizations, and citizens will interact with AI to synthesize evidence, understand the problems, propose solutions, evaluate alternatives, and model the entire institutional and organizational architecture to policy implementation.

This dynamic occurs in a broader dimension of policy advice. It also occurs in a micro dimension, in which AI creates evidence, information, and knowledge that influences policy practice among street-level bureaucrats. For example, using predictive policing in security policies radically changes how security agents act in society. Predictive policing involves collecting a broad variety of data to estimate, through several correlations, when and where crime is likely to occur, thereby more efficiently employing existing resources to avoid it (O'Neil, 2016; Meijer & Wessels, 2019). Usually, machine learning makes predictions by artificial neural networks that shape police action. In public security, AI advises on micro actions fundamental to policy implementation, which changes the relationships between governments and citizens.

AI transforms the entire logic of policy advice, both in a macro sense, in the dynamics of formulation, and in a micro sense, shifting the implementation actions. Considering the way instrument constituencies act in the design of AI instruments, their deployment as an essential knowledge structure in implementation changes political decision-making's entire composition and public action's construction in society. Transforming policy advice's structure means having AI instruments that change the knowledge dynamics of policymakers, in turn changing the outcomes of interventions and the impact on society.

4.3 Coda: AI Disruption in Policy Knowledge

AI in the policy process is a transversal knowledge policy instrument. This perspective challenges the foundations of policy science because AI transforms the way policy analysts produce knowledge, and it has practical consequences.

AI is integrated throughout the policy cycle, creating knowledge about problems and the policymaking. AI is a knowledge instrument that is transversal to all other policy instruments, requiring that its integration be dependent on a new type of policy work: data modeling and algorithms for AI systems.

The transformations in policy work arise from interactions between policymakers and AI systems, adding a new layer to the policy cycle. On the one hand, policymakers participate in the modeling of AI systems, participating in instrument constituencies to solve problems. On the other hand, policymakers utilize the knowledge generated from these AI models to address problems of varying magnitudes, amplifying knowledge for policy formulation and evaluation, and automating elements and actions of implementation.

From a positivist perspective, we have the idea that policy scientists no longer produce knowledge. The idea that machines manipulate and operate policy knowledge creates a techno-solutionist imaginary, often present in Lasswell's ideas (1970). On the other hand, the integration of AI reproduces many of the problems associated with muddling through (Lindblom, 1959). In contexts where AI is integrated into the policy process, it does not change the bounded rationality, causing this integration to reproduce the idea that policies are incremental and driven by trial and error. The integration of AI constitutes machines of muddling through, in which knowledge is constituted without clarity of policy objectives, creating difficulties in the policy decision-making process.

In many situations, the integration of AI into the policy process creates new opportunities for mixed scanning (Etzioni, 1968). AI enables a broad review of the decision-making field without requiring a detailed analysis of each alternative. This review enables the examination of alternatives created by prediction or simulation, leading to informed decision-making. Finally, the use of AI in the policy process challenges a critical perspective, as it creates discursive frames, particularly with generative AI (Oder & Béland, 2025). The disruption of AI in public policy lies in its integration into policy analysis.

The disruption occurs in the foundations of policy knowledge because the use of AI throughout the policy process modifies the foundations of policy analysis. First, we have the pillar of knowledge in data and the construction of knowledge through sophisticated mathematical models (Floridi, 2023b). Even when we consider texts and speeches within critical policy studies as empirical objects, the use of generative AI creates new possibilities in the treatment of data and the construction of policymakers' action frames. Second, disruption occurs because prediction and simulation become central to this dynamic, enabling the creation of fast machines to generate scenarios, predict problems, and inform solutions. Third, disruption occurs because AI becomes integrated as an automation tool, modifying the entire organizational structure where policymakers operate. In short, disruption occurs because humans and machines interact to generate policy knowledge and perform policy work.

The development and application of AI in policy demands that policymakers take actions to frame and outline AI policies, with special attention to issues of transparency, accountability, and responsibility. In this sense, modeling must adopt a series of procedures and instruments that we will analyze in the following section. AI applied in policy processes has an infinite range of recommendations for the action of policymakers, bureaucrats, citizens, and companies in contexts of decision-making and collective action. As previously highlighted, integrating AI in policy processes has risks and limitations, including data quality, algorithmic architecture choices framing, and development and coding in complex political contexts. AI changes the practice and scientific approach to public policy because it changes the knowledge structure and the situations, frames, and scripts for the policy action. Given AI's limitations, problems, and risks, governance mechanisms for policies modeled with AI are necessary, which we will analyze in the next section.

5 Governing AI in the Policy Cycle

As AI increasingly becomes integrated into the future of governance, its transformative powers offer enticing possibilities. Yet we also must contemplate the multiple governance challenges that AI invokes, which are central to the policy process. Procedures for technological governance are required for AI in policy process, if it is an instrument. AI in policy process shapes risks and problems, demanding frameworks for its design and development, and how it produces knowledge that implies government action. AI applied in public policy has consequences for people's lives, with diverse economic, social, political, and cultural impacts. AI in public policy means government organizations adopting AI to generate knowledge that supports action through opaque, uncertain, and ambiguous technologies. Framing a governance perspective of AI applied in public policy and defining the instruments through which this governance will become operational is essential for developing AI-based government technologies.

5.1 Ethical Dilemmas and AI in the Policy Cycle

Digital technologies' advancement tends to create an imaginative vision of greater political neutrality and accuracy of public decisions based on data (Esko & Koulu, 2023). Using AI in public policy is surrounded by an imagined world of policies implemented in a faster, more effective, safer, and more neutral way. AI applied in policy enables imagination to augmenting the productivity of public service and benefits for society. This imaginary place creates a tech-solutionist frame for AI in public policy, where we rely on and pursue using technology as the foremost solution, without heeding the social and political dilemmas that emerge. For example, in 2019, the Dutch government's tax authority used AI based on a machine learning algorithm to create risk profiles to spot fraud among people applying for childcare benefits. In practice, this AI would recommend to bureaucrats whether families would be eligible to receive the benefit. Thus, authorities penalized families over a mere suspicion of fraud based on the system's risk indicators. Tens of thousands of families were pushed into poverty because of exorbitant debts to the tax agency. Reports indicate that some victims committed suicide. The scandal resulted in more than a thousand children being taken into foster care (Newman & Mintrom, 2023).

This case of the Dutch government demonstrates how AI can incur ethical dilemmas from the perspective of its use and application in the policy process. This techno-solutionist vision provides a frame of opaque technologies that infuse human actions by defining individual and collective choices. Within human-machine interactions, these frames are constructed discursively and based on ideas and values that make AI-based instruments ambiguous and powerful in defining action (Khanal, Zhang & Taeihagh, 2025). The Dutch government's goal was to reinforce austerity policies and improve the provision of public benefits with the moral duty of fairness and honesty. It is not possible to discuss here whether the Dutch government acted well or badly. The fact is that the use of technologies is driven by discursive frames that instill values and norms into the use of technologies (Mendonça, Filgueiras & Almeida, 2023).

The sociotechnical reengineering of public policy has a series of implications for society and the political system, centering debate around the use of AI as a complex set of social dilemmas, normally discussed from a risk perspective. A social dilemma is a situation of interdependence between people in which there is conflict between doing what is best for oneself versus what is best for the group. The social dilemmas of AI in public policy emerge from human-machine interactions and the mode of how algorithms institutionalize policy practices and knowledge. By delegating the task of solving problems and making decisions to an AI, a false image is created that social dilemmas in public policies have been overcome. Sociotechnical reengineering of public policy with AI produces social dilemmas because of ethical issues.

The first dilemma is epistemological. AI introduces a dilemma related to its predictive power and how it resonates with human action. Deploying AI in a policy cycle has the goal of predicting and simulating all decision-making and tasks. According to Nowotny, we use AI to increase our control over the future and uncertainty, while AI's performativity – the power it has to make us act in the way it predicts – reduces our agency over the future (Nowotny, 2021). The way policymakers delegate to AI the power to decide and perform tasks reduces the margin of human control over technology. AI creates the sense that public policy governance is data-driven and neutral. However, algorithmic governance does not supplant democracy because of an epistemic impossibility. Even if AI were to exercise algorithmic governance, it would not supplant democracy because humans continue to construct data and information that feed decision-making (Innerarity, 2024).

The spectrum of complexity and uncertainties in public policy means that defining problems and constructing solutions depends on a new type of knowledge, which is comprehensive and uncertain, yet granular and focused on individuals. However, the modeling policy work based on AI imposes many challenges for governments in designing and implementing effective policies to govern AI. We do not fully understand the problems posed by AI, which makes the technology itself unpredictable, intractable, and nonlinear, making it onerous for governments to create an institutional framework and correct objectives for their policies (Gasser & Almeida, 2017).

The second dilemma is controlling technology. Not knowing the problems and uncertainties related to AI makes the paths forward ambiguous, as we expect greater knowledge with AI's deployment in public policy, while at the same time we do not know its dynamics for producing knowledge. Social dilemmas arise in the way in which the framing of AI in public policy implies interventions in human life, without us having control over it (Russell, 2019). An example of this issue of control is the discussion on lethal autonomous weapons (LAW) at the United Nations Office for Disarmament Affairs. AI is embarked in drones and robots that search for, identify, and eliminate targets autonomously, without human intervention (Russell et al., 2022). The United Nations creates debates on banning LAW. However, these debates were hampered by veto issues from countries that are major players in this technology, particularly the United States, Israel, China, and Russia. Recently, the Lavender system, a LAW developed by Israel, was widely used in the conflict in Gaza. Lavender was developed to identify people linked to Hamas or Jihad, with an accuracy of 90%. There are reports that the use of Lavender in Gaza resulted in the elimination of civilian targets in their homes, which were systematically bombed.[2]

---

[2] www.972mag.com/lavender-ai-israeli-army-gaza/.

Because AI significantly reduces human control over decisions, it creates new challenges for ascribing responsibility and legal liability for AI's harms imposed on others. AI is a technology that learns and adapts to the environment by following the rules set out in algorithms, without humans being able to control the results and impose responsibility on systems. So, the unpredictability of machine learning-based decisions implies that many erroneous decisions made by AI are beyond the control of and cannot be anticipated by society (Lim & Taeihagh, 2019).

The ethical challenge of AI in public policy concerns the extent to which governments can construct interventions in society, prioritizing people's lives, while using technologies whose decisions are unpredictable and uncertain. These decisions are subject to diverse forms of algorithmic injustice (Eubanks, 2018), invisibility of identities or visibility of prejudice (Noble, 2018), or even policy failures that cause harm in society. The Dutch case is an example in which the harms caused by AI create ethical dilemmas and require innovations in governance processes that go beyond traditional patterns in policy theory. The ethical dilemma of the Dutch case lies in the fact that wanting to do the right thing with AI – regardless of what we think is right or wrong – produces unforeseen effects on society, making it necessary to have a governance framework that is also uncertain and experimental.

The epistemological dilemma posed by Nowotny (2021) extends into uncertainties and the way in which delegating decisions to an AI system produces consequences for society. According to Floridi, the world of AI produces a divorce between agency and intelligence. Epistemologically, AI as a new form of agency can be harnessed ethically and unethically (Floridi, 2023b). When AI is applied throughout the policy process, this divorce is amplified. On the one hand, it produces epistemic changes in policy work, in which policymakers, bureaucrats, citizens, and corporations delegate decision-making and task performance to AI systems, changing the entire policy advisory system and forging actors' actions shaped with an artificial (rather than a properly human) intelligence. Within the interactions between humans and machines in the policy process, AI as an epistemic instrument can be modeled and deployed ethically and unethically. In this sense, faced with the ethical dilemmas of AI, we need governance frameworks that make it possible to instill practices and procedures that ensure ethical AI development.

AI governance in public policy starts from principles that frame AI development and deployment to governments and companies, creating a discursive and normative frame. AI ethics require principles that guide innovation and technological deployment. AI ethics do not have a consensus about the principles. However, international organizations such as the Organization for Economic

Co-operation and Development (OECD) disclose and disseminate principles. The AI principles from OECD include:

- inclusive growth, sustainable development, and well-being;
- human rights and democratic values, including fairness and privacy;
- transparency and explainability;
- robustness, security, and safety; and
- accountability.

AI principles are not a "one size fits all" approach, but rather action guidelines that frame institutional arrangements to governance. Similarly, organizations such as UNESCO advocate an ethical perspective on AI that is grounded in strengthening democracy. The cornerstone of the United Nations Educational, Scientific and Cultural Organization's (UNESCO's) "Recommendation on the Ethics of Artificial Intelligence" is the advancement of fundamental principles such as transparency and fairness, while always remembering the importance of human oversight for AI systems. The principles formulated by UNESCO comprise a framework for AI development aimed at the following:

- *Proportionality and do no harm*: the use of AI systems should not go beyond what is necessary to achieve a legitimate objective. Risk assessment should be used to avoid harm that may result from such uses.
- *Safety and security*: unintended harm (security risks) as well as vulnerabilities to attacks should be prevented and addressed by AI actors.
- *Right to privacy and data protection*: privacy should be protected and promoted throughout the AI lifecycle. Adequate data protection frameworks should also be established.
- *Collaborative, adaptive, and multistakeholder governance*: international law and national sovereignty should be respected in the use of data. Furthermore, multistakeholder engagement is necessary for inclusive approaches to AI governance.
- *Responsibility and accountability*: AI systems should be auditable and traceable. There should be oversight, impact assessment, auditing, and due diligence mechanisms in place to avoid conflicts with human rights standards and threats to environmental well-being.
- *Transparency and explainability*: AI systems' ethical deployment depends on their transparency and explainability (T&E). The level of T&E should be appropriate to the context, as there may be tensions between T&E and other principles such as privacy, safety, and security.
- *Human oversight and determination*: Member States should ensure that AI systems do not displace ultimate human responsibility and accountability.

- *Sustainability*: AI technologies should be assessed against their impact on sustainability, understood as a set of evolving goals, including those set out in the United Nations Sustainable Development Goals.
- *Awareness and literacy*: Public understanding of AI and data should be promoted through open and accessible education, civic engagement, digital skills training and AI ethics, and media and information literacy.
- *Fairness and non-discrimination*: AI actors should promote social justice, impartiality, and non-discrimination, while adopting an inclusive approach to ensure that the benefits of AI are accessible to all.

From this frame, AI ethics guides on the reflection of human-machine interactions, in which the discussion on the moral status of AI is essential. The AI ethics framework addresses the moral implications of AI to society, assessing the moral status of AI instruments and their social, economic, cultural, and political effects. The principles guide human action to design AI systems and the working of these systems in human-machine interactions. AI ethics' primary claim is that humans create mechanisms and instruments to control AI. This claim is appropriate to public policy, in which the technological deployment is challenging and disruptive. The main claim translates these principles into practical action to create governance instruments for AI in public policy. Likewise, it creates mechanisms that assign humans in control, especially in public policy. Keeping humans abreast of AI deployment in the policy cycle is the main challenge in public policy, as the mode of knowledge created by AI shapes human behavior and government action.

5.2 Humans in the Loop and AI Governance in the Policy Cycle

Next, we consider the *humans-in-the-loop* approach, which reframes an automation problem from human–machine interactions (Amershi et al., 2014). Reframing an automation problem means that humans create controls on AI to calibrate outcomes and to involve humans in the system design. The application of the humans-in-the-loop approach perspective in public policy is that humans calibrate AI instruments by exercising supervision and controlling the flow of input data, and then evaluating the output data's outcomes and impacts. Humans-in-the-loop approach enables an innovative way of calibrating policy instruments when AI is integrated into the policy cycle. Similar to traditional policy instruments, humans can calibrate the instruments so that they are more reliable in achieving policy objectives.

The humans-in-the-loop is an approach that instrumentalizes by governance the calibrations of outcomes and designing and redesigning the AI systems. In AI-shaped public policy, the humans-in-the-loop approach means that humans can calibrate both the design of systems and the constituency of AI-based policy instruments, on the one hand, and the outcomes of systems that reorganize policy advice. This means that the humans-in-the-loop approach meets the instrument constituencies, requiring compliance with procedures such as transparency, open training databases, or privacy and data protection. Meanwhile, the humans-in-the-loop approach also meets the systems outcomes, providing procedures that require algorithmic audits, system validation, or regulatory sandboxes in a democratic frame.

Naturally, this approach demands governance instruments, which are experimental and emerging in the policy landscape. Calibrations from human feedback are essential to develop AI in public policy, as AI systems are based on machine learning algorithms that adapt to their users and environment. Guided by the AI principles, humans can calibrate outcomes and review the entire dynamics of AI systems in the policy landscape. The humans-in-the-loop approach and AI governance emerge from AI regulations delivered recently by governments. Contexts of uncertainty and profound technological change shape emerging regulatory and governance approaches.

The European Union Artificial Intelligence Act, for example, requires that AI designers allow human control to achieve effective human oversight. Under article 14, AI systems should be designed in a path that can be overseen by people in the AI lifecycle. The objective is to formulate policies to compel AI designers to integrate the human control function as part of the safeguard against AI risks and malfunctions. The EU AI Act develops a regulatory approach based on the risks of AI. It defines a framework of rights that allows humans to request a review of decisions made by AI systems, as well as transparency and control requirements. Based on the risks, AI systems are classified as low, limited, high, and unacceptable risk. Based on this classification of an AI system, there are different requirements for different rights. Low-risk AI, such as video games or spam filters, requires AI developers to follow codes of conduct. Limited-risk AI, such as chatbots or deepfakes, implies transparency requirements. High-risk AI, such as those applied in educational processes, requires compliance and algorithmic impact assessments. Finally, unacceptable-risk AI, such as social scoring or facial recognition, is prohibited under European legislation. Each country in the European Community defines a national authority to enforce the AI Act, and a central authority coordinates all activities. The European Union prioritizes its norms or rather its market power (Ulnicane, 2022).

China, in contrast, takes a state command-and-control approach to AI regulation and governance. China's emerging regulation is based on central planning by the State Council, which outlines a timeline and strategy to advance AI development and build out AI regulations in China. In addition, the State Council has established an expert group to draft a law that aims to promote innovation in AI technology, develop a healthy AI industry, and regulate AI products and services. It contains provisions for managing AI systems, safeguarding national security and public interest, and protecting the rights and interests of individuals and organizations. In addition, there are several recommendations, such as the one from the China Academy of Information and Communications Technology on building trustworthy AI. In addition, there are specific recommendations on the development of generative AI. This emerging command-and-control perspective in China signifies the state's ability to provide regulatory instruments based on direct command to developers, with oversight by the State Council (Liu, Zhang & Sui, 2024).

In the United States, there is no comprehensive legislation on AI regulation. The regulatory approach in the United States is built around self-regulation, infusing voluntary guidelines and best practices for AI systems, reflecting a cautious approach to regulation aimed at fostering innovation without imposing strict mandates. In this framework, the US government is concerned about losing competitiveness with China in the AI market, fragmenting legislative proposals into topics such as copyright, AI in education, AI robocalls, biological risks, and AI's role in national security. In general, the perspective of self-regulation in the United States is based on the idea that users can calibrate AI outcomes, opening the technology to direct intervention by society. Regulation in the United States is far from the need for empowered authorities to impose rules on the constitution and use of AI-based systems in different social sectors (Judge, Nitzberg & Russell, 2025).

These emerging perspectives on AI regulation and governance hope to enable human control over AI, so these approaches sound uncertain in contexts of profound technological change. Humans-in-the-loop approach frames AI governance. Creating human control over AI is essential to align technologies and human objectives. Alignment issues in AI emerge when assessing the performance of an AI in normative terms. Alignment is the normative non-anomalous AI behaviour with or without the incorporation of human workers and users in these operations (Gabriel, 2020). Alignment lies in the fact that an AI can respect the foundational principles of technological development, such as those disseminated by UNESCO and the OECD.

With alignment issues and emerging regulatory frameworks on the horizon, three challenges are foundational to AI governance, particularly when applied in the public policy cycle. First, information asymmetries between people and instrument constituencies. Instrument constituencies engage in AI development and deployment in a policy context shaped by information asymmetries.

Second, the lack of normative consensus increases the complexity of technology control and obscures AI's potential. Third, the government mismatches the design of effective, efficient, and legitimate means (strategies, approaches, tools, and so forth) to resolve the substantive issues, concerning the conditions of uncertainty and complexity in the AI ecosystem. Governments have failed to design policies regarding AI because of the limits on traditional approaches to law and policymaking in the digital age (Gasser & Almeida, 2017).

AI governance is structured in layers, with different problems and approaches. The technical, ethical, social, and legal layers put in the AI landscape are challenges to institutionalized governance for emerging technologies deployed in the policy cycle. From here, AI governance proceeds in two ways: first, AI is a substantial instrument in the policy cycle applied in policy formulation, implementation, and evaluation; second, AI governance requires a set of procedural instruments that steer the mode of constituencies and design dynamics, adaptation to the institutional framework, alignment with ethical principles, accountability, transparency, and technical requirements. Procedural instruments, typical in AI governance, are used to indirectly but significantly affect policy processes and outcomes (Bali et al., 2021). In the different layers that comprise AI governance, all instruments are procedural, with the objective being to steer actions and organizations to govern emerging technologies. Table 2 offers a synthesis of procedures concerning all layers of AI governance.

AI governance in public policy is about procedures concerning ethical, technical, and regulatory requirements to assign humans in the loop with technologies that make decisions and conduct tasks in the policy process. Thus, AI governance in public policy is about defining who can do what when, where, and how with requirements to action to align AI with government objectives, democracy, and public values (Korinek & Balwit, 2023; Innerarity, 2024). Integrating the main layers of AI governance is essential to align technology development and social good (Wirtz, Weyerer & Sturm, 2020). AI governance's procedural logic is asserted by the necessity to maintain humans in the loop with AI applied in the policy process. The main objective is designing an institutional framework that integrates ethical, technical, and social and regulatory layers (Gasser & Almeida, 2017), delivering procedural instruments that create a logic of appropriateness for AI development (Filgueiras, 2022b). Between the procedural instruments for AI governance, Table 2 enumerates the main instruments applied to AI development and deployment. Data governance procedural instruments, such as interoperability, data sharing, data collection, and qualification are essential to AI in public policy. In the same vein, regulatory procedural instruments such as sandboxes

Table 2 AI governance's layers and procedural instruments in the policy landscape.

Layers of AI governance	Topic	Procedural instruments
Ethical	Principles	Code of ethics
	People	Courses and training for public servants
		Guides for developing inclusive AI
		National AI strategy
	Constituencies	Centers of excellence and innovation in AI
		Common development framework
		Cooperation with universities
		Coordination
		Political support
		Transparency
Technical	Data governance	Data assessment and exclusion in public databases
		Data collection
		Data qualification
		Data sharing
		Interoperability
		Open data policy
		Opening system training databases
	Algorithmic accountability	Responsibility ecosystems
		AI oversight and control agency
		Algorithmic audits
		Algorithmic risk allocations
		Public algorithm registries
	Standards	AI development toolkits
		Cybersecurity infrastructures
		Standardization of algorithm selection
		Standardization of technical documentation
		System validation
		Training database standards
Social and legal	Norms	Principles
		Rights
	Regulation	Periodic assessment of AI systems
		Regulatory sandboxes
		Privacy and data protection
		Intellectual property

Source: Gasser & Almeida (2017) and own elaboration.

or privacy and protection are essential to align AI with social goods. Finally, defining ethical principles and codes of conduct for AI designers and developers is essential to create a public value perspective.

The challenge of AI governance is that the procedural instruments are beyond the government. The AI governance landscape requires approaches that are beyond governments' power to regulate and define procedures. Another alignment in AI governance is a global digital ecosystem with local needs and institutions. For example, diverse AI are designed and deployed in cloud systems, without government capacities to regulate and impose control (Filgueiras & Almeida, 2021). In AI governance, the institutional framework to define rules and procedures to develop and deploy AI systems is labeled in a multistakeholder perspective. From this perspective, the objective is to couple global and local institutions with emerging practices to govern AI. The challenge is that humans supervise decisions and tasks performed by AI and then create a perspective that evolves and creates knowledge from human feedback framed in data, controls, and regulations. Yet the humans in the loop approach involves the micro and macro institutions (Table 3).

The macro level concerns more global and systemic norms and practices, which require multistakeholder constructions to define technical standards, internationally shared norms and rights, and frameworks for governance. At the micro level, AI governance deals with institutionalizing principles and how they translate into practical action. Similarly, at the micro level, it deals with how reciprocal feedback between humans and machines will be processed and how humans supervise systems' work. The micro level deals with institutionalizing practices related to compliance with fundamental procedures that need to be performed by developers, companies, governments, and other organizations.

Table 3 Layers and levels of AI governance.

Level	Layers		
	Ethical	Technical	Social & regulatory
Micro	Principles that shape AI development	Reciprocal feedback between humans and machines	Humans supervise
Macro	Frameworks to governance	Standards and rules	Norms and rights

Source: own elaboration.

In the human–machine interactions, AI governance is essential to policy process. The challenge is how to govern disruptive technologies with large uncertainty and ambiguities. AI governance requires a policy perspective based on procedural instruments to align technological development in the policy process and outcomes in terms of policy knowledge, practices, ideas, analyses, and work. This challenge is strange – to create a policy environment adapted to disruptive AI technologies applied in policy process. Policymakers and bureaucrats have limited knowledge concerning how it works and why, as well as what the possible applications and consequences are for its deployment. Furthermore, policymakers and bureaucrats have a policy environment shaped by uncertainty and structural power dynamics framed by big techs (Taeihagh, Ramesh & Howlett, 2021). AI in policy cycle and structural power dynamics creates a governance context based on uncertainty, making it difficult for governments to design policies and regulatory perspectives.

6 Concluding Remarks

AI's development and deployment in public policy is quite broad, encompassing the entire policy cycle. The condition for AI to make decisions or perform some policy tasks is to have large volumes of data, computing power, human developers, and interfaces that enable constant interaction between humans and machines to perform actions throughout the policy cycle.

The integration of AI into public policy means ushering in an epistocratic style of policy process, creating the fantasy that machines can make decisions for humans and perform diverse tasks in the context of governments. AI in public policy represents a form of instrumental rationalism that is dedicated to data-driven decision-making. This emerging instrumental rationalism is insulated from political contestation and from contexts where actors struggle with wicked problems. AI can be an excellent instrument to accelerate the production of knowledge. However, it fails to align itself with the narrative and critical frames that emerge in society (Hartley & Kuecker, 2022).

AI, especially in the field of public policy, demands a broad governance process to frame technological development in procedures and rules that aim at effectiveness, safety, and create action scripts to align technology with public value. As a knowledge instrument, it has the potential to be a factor in organizational rationalization and produce profound epistemic changes in the policy process. However, this is no guarantee that we will have a rational, neutral, and effective policy process. The social and political dilemmas of public policy remain from the moment that AI integration in public policy follows a logic of instrument constituency, and its development is permeated by interests, opinions, and perspectives on which solution is best at a given moment. Throughout the policy cycle, AI is a solution looking for problems, with a view to the production of systems on an industrial scale, framed in a techno-solutionist perspective that changes how decisions are made and tasks are performed in an unpredictable way.

On the one hand, AI in the policy process opens a range of opportunities, working as a mechanism capable of identifying problems and providing feedback from society in real-time, enabling governments to adjust their policies according to the agendas that emerge in society. Furthermore, AI can automate repetitive activities in the implementation process and work as a rationalizing mechanism for public organizations. Likewise, it is possible to automate the entire evaluation process, aligning public policies with public values. In all these circumstances, the opportunities that AI opens represent profound changes in the policy process. Its ability to create knowledge with large volumes of data quickly, augmented, and effectively shifts the government's work. AI creates new epistemologies and affordances for policymakers to act in the public sphere.

On the other hand, AI poses a series of risks when governments become dependent on it to perform their agency in society. The possibilities of exclusion, invisibility of populations, organizational risks, ethical failures, and technological dependence challenge governments to transform their structures by investing in infrastructure and computing power. The possibilities for public policies to be governed in an epistocratic manner are great, directly impacting the functioning of democratic regimes. AI represents an opaque technology, which brings new difficulties for accountability and demands new governance mechanisms.

This duality of AI in public policy requires actions on the part of policymakers. First, aligning the integration of AI into the policy process with the broader public values of a democracy (Mendonça, Filgueiras & Almeida, 2023). In addition, policymakers need to establish governance frameworks that facilitate human oversight of the advancement of AI (Russell, 2019; Straub et al., 2023; Mergel et al., 2023). The adoption of AI in governments needs alignment with a governance framework in operational, knowledge, and normative works (Straub et al., 2023). Third, observe the international issues involved with the advancement of AI. AI requires global governance mechanisms due to international data flows, the global nature of the Internet, and the need for economic policies aimed at breaking global monopolies by big tech companies (Tallberg et al., 2023).

The disruption caused by AI lies in the way it shakes the functioning of the government machine in the dimension of its actors and institutions. AI's increasing pervasiveness throughout the policy cycle means that system design actions intertwine with typical actions for policy formulation, implementation, and evaluation. This intertwining creates a higher layer, in which the design of AI systems becomes actions for designing policy in the context of uncertainty, ambiguity, and opacity that are framed within the political system's broader context. Designing an AI system with the goal of automating and augmenting a public policy represents a political activity at the moment objectives are being outlined, resources are being allocated, instruments are being defined to achieve the objectives, and the system's deployment is putting the policy into implementation.

Artificial intelligence does not change the dilemmas for decision-making and policy design. The political and social dilemmas remain the same, but with different practices, involving a data-driven language, algorithmic architectures, logical and abstract system design, operation, and implementation. Overall, policy work transforms as actors begin to interact with AI to perform actions based on a radical and abrupt change in the structure of knowledge in society. Working with large volumes of data – within systems that deliver information in real time and that automate repetitive tasks – causes the focus of policy work to change. Humans interact with systems applied in public policy by offering data and information, an abstract logic of systems, and objectives. On the other hand, AI systems return information and actions that optimize various elements of the policy process. Furthermore, it modifies the entire structure of policy advisory, creating new patterns of action, new ways of understanding problems, and shaping solutions that aim to achieve a political objective.

Artificial intelligence does not overcome the set of political activities circumscribed in the frames that surround its defense and hype, as well as its criticisms and identification of threats that technological advances pose to governments. In the field of public policy, understanding AI's construction and use must be thought of in a more realistic and effective framework. AI is not a solution to all problems nor is it a neutral technology that automatically provides effective changes. Adopting AI in the policy process requires legitimacy, given the constitutive dilemmas of any public policy, such as effectiveness, efficiency, security, and achieving public purposes. Likewise, AI is not an existential threat to humanity. Framing the discussion is extremely important, and AI should be thought of in a framework focused on its instrumental character, associated with its possibilities of use and challenges that involve its development and construction.

Conceived as an instrument of knowledge within the policy process, AI, however, produces a series of changes in policy work. Science and evidence are commonly seen as the epistemic building blocks of rationalist policymaking. Accordingly, the Lasswellian vision of policy science has democracy embodying the romanticized image of a professional moving between scientific and political realms. The fact is that AI does not mean the most "scientific," evidence-based policymaking. AI systems are created by trial and error in uncertain contexts and with opaque technologies, driven by a metric of accuracy to solve a problem or perform a task. AI is a valuable tool for producing organizational optimization. However, it produces a series of new problems that require human oversight, governance frameworks, and new modes of policy work to deal with emerging issues, such as algorithmic unfairness, security issues, or threats.

The professional field of policy science must absorb a new capacity related to the development of systems. It also must absorb new ways of dealing with the knowledge created by AI systems applied in various areas of the policy cycle. AI systems are knowledge systems that transform the practical action of policy analysts and practitioners. The epistemic changes that emerge with AI transform all policy work, underpinning new rationalities, frameworks, and action scripts that transform the way to effective policies. On the one hand, policy work must be attentive to system design processes, considering the dynamics of instrument constituency. On the other hand, AI is an instrument to accelerate and increase policy analysis and to influence new patterns of action through prediction and simulation.

In the context of these epistemic changes, the disruptive changes in policy science impact the way governments understand their problems, formulate and implement solutions, and evaluate them. The risk is that policymakers and implementers delegate analytical capacities to AI systems to predict the future, while at the same time these policymakers and implementers lose control over the future. These risks require governments to rethink problems and solutions and create initiatives that are capable of adapting AI to the complex reality of policy, both in terms of knowledge construction and analysis, and from a professional perspective. At the same time, we must face a totalizing and epistocratic perspective of public policy formulated and implemented with AI. This is the main challenge, which calls on policy scientists to think about sociotechnical reengineering in a broader framework of defense of democracy and its virtues, in a broader scenario of defense of freedom and human autonomy.

References

Acemoglu, D. (2024). The simple macroeconomics of AI. Working paper – National Bureau of Economic Research, 32487. https://doi.org/10.3386/w32487.

Ahn, M. J., Chen, Y. C. (2022). Digital transformation toward AI-augmented public administration: The perception of government employees and the willingness to use AI in government. *Government Information Quarterly*, 39(2), 101664. https://doi.org/10.1016/j.giq.2021.101664.

Allahyari, M., Pouriyeh, S., Assefi, M., et al. (2017). A brief survey of text mining: Classification, clustering and extraction techniques. *Arxiv*. https://doi.org/10.48550/arXiv.1707.02919.

Alon-Barkat, S., Busuioc, M. (2023). Human–AI interactions in public sector decision making: "Automation bias" and "selective adherence" to algorithmic advice. *Journal of Public Administration Research and Theory*, 33(1), 153–169. https://doi.org/10.1093/jopart/muac007.

Althaus, M. (2013). Reflections on advisory practice in politics. *PSCA— Political Science Applied*, 2, 5–15.

Alvarado, R. (2023). AI as an epistemic technology. *Science Engineering Ethics*, 29, 1–30. https://doi.org/10.1007/s11948-023-00451-3.

Amershi, S., Cakmak, M., Knox, W. B., Kulesza, T. (2014). Power to the people: The role of humans in interactive machine learning. *AI Magazine*, 35(4), 105–120. https://doi.org/10.1609/aimag.v35i4.2513.

Amoore, L. (2024). The deep border. Political Geography, 109, 102547. https://doi.org/10.1016/j.polgeo.2021.102547.

Amoore, L. (2022). Machine learning political orders. *Review of International Studies*, 49(1), 20–36. https://doi.org/10.1017/S0260210522000031.

Amoore, L. (2014). Security and the incalculable. *Security Dialogue*, 45(5), 423–439. http://dx.doi.org/10.1177/0967010614539719.

Anthony, C. (2021). When knowledge work and analytical technologies collide: The practices and consequences of black boxing algorithmic technologies. *Administrative Science Quarterly*, 66(4), 1173–1212. https://doi.org/10.1177/00018392211016755.

Anthony, J. B. (2020) Managing digital transformation of smart cities through enterprise architecture – a review and research agenda. *Enterprise Information Systems*, 15(3), 299–331. https://doi.org/10.1080/17517575.2020.1812006.

References

Arcas, B. A. (2024). The birth and rebirth of AI, in Lane, M., Sethumadhavan, A. (eds.), *Collaborative Intelligence: How Humans and AI are Transforming our World*. Cambridge, MA: MIT Press, 21–31.

Bali, A. S., Howlett, M., Lewis, J. M., Ramesh, M. (2021). Procedural policy tools in theory and practice. *Policy and Society*, 40(3), 295–311. https://doi.org/10.1080/14494035.2021.1965379.

Banuri, S., Dercon, S., Gauri, V. (2019). Biased policy professionals. *The World Bank Economic Review*, 33(2), 310–327. https://doi.org/10.1093/wber/lhy033.

Barandiaran, X., Di Paolo, E., Rohde, M. (2009). Defining agency: Individuality, normativity, asymmetry and spatial temporality in action. *Adaptive Behaviour*, 17(5), 367–386.

Bardach, E. (2012). *A Practical Guide for Policy Analysis: The Eightfold Path to More Effective Problem Solving*. Los Angeles: Sage.

Barzelay, M. (2019). *Public Management as a Design-Oriented Professional Discipline*. Cheltenham: Edward-Elgar.

Baumgartner, F. R., Jones, B. D. (2015). *The Politics of Information: Problem Definition and the Course of Public Policy in America*. Chicago. The University of Chicago Press.

Béland, D. (2019). *How Ideas and Institutions Shape Politics and Policy*. Cambridge: Cambridge University Press.

Béland, D., Howlett, M. (2016). Instrument constituencies in the policy process. *Governance*, 29(3), 393–409. https://doi.org/10.1111/gove.12179.

Bender, E. M., Gebru, T., McMillan-Major, A., Shmitchell, S. (2021). On the dangers of stochastic parrots: Can language models be too big? In: *Proceedings of the 2021 ACM Conference on Fairness, Accountability, and Transparency (FAccT '21)*. New York: Association for Computing Machinery, 610–623. https://doi.org/10.1145/3442188.3445922.

Bengio, Y. (2023). AI and catastrophic risk. *Journal of Democracy*, 34(4), 111–121.

Benjamin, R. (2019). *Race after Technology: Abolitionist Tools for the New Jim Code*. New York: Polity Press.

Blumer, H. (1986). *Symbolic Interactionism: Perspective and Method*. Berkeley: University of California Press.

Bovens, M., 't Hart, P., Kuipers, S. (2008). The politics of policy evaluation, in Goodin, R., Moran, M., Rein. M (eds.), *The Oxford Handbook of Public Policy* Oxford: Oxford University Press, 319–335.

Braunerhjelm, P., Hepburn, C. (2023). Climate change, complexity, and policy design. *Oxford Review of Economic Policy*, 39(4), 667–679. https://doi.org/10.1093/oxrep/grad047.

Braybrooke, D., Lindblom, C. E. (1963). *A Strategy of Decision*. New York: Free Press.

Brennan, J. (2016). *Against Democracy*. Princeton: Princeton University Press.

Buolamwini, J. (2023). *Unmasking AI: My Mission to Protect What Is Human in a World of Machines*. New York: Random House.

Campion, A., Gasco-Hernandez, M., Jankin Mikhaylov, S., Esteve, M. (2022). Overcoming the challenges of collaboratively adopting artificial intelligence in the public sector. *Social Science Computer Review*, 40(2), 462–477. https://doi.org/10.1177/0894439320979953.

Capano, G., Howlett, M. P. (2020). The knowns and unknowns of policy instrument analysis: Policy tools and the current research agenda on policy mixes. *SAGE Open*, 10(1), 1–13. https://doi.org/10.1177/2158244019900568.

Capano, G., Malandrino, A. (2022). Mapping the use of knowledge in policy-making: Barriers and facilitators from a subjectivist perspective (1990–2020). *Policy Sciences*, 55, 399–428. https://doi.org/10.1007/s11077-022-09468-0.

Chaqués-Bonafont, L., Palau, A. M., Baumgartner, F. (2015). *Agenda Dynamics in Spain*. London: Palgrave.

Chatfield, A. T., Reddick, C. G. (2019). A framework for Internet of Things-enabled smart government: A case of IoT cybersecurity policies and use cases in U.S. federal government. *Government Information Quarterly*, 36(2), 346–357. https://doi.org/10.1016/j.giq.2018.09.007.

Chen, C., Surette, R., and Shah, M. (2021). Automated monitoring for security camera networks: Promise from computer vision labs. *Security Journal*, 34, 389–409. https://doi.org/10.1057/s41284-020-00230-w.

Clifton, J., Pal, L. A. (2022). The policy dilemmas of blockchain, *Policy and Society*, 41(3), 321–327. https://doi.org/10.1093/polsoc/puac025.

Coeckelbergh, M. (2021). Narrative responsibility and artificial intelligence: How AI changes human responsibility and sense making. *AI & Society*, 38(4), 2437–2450. https://doi.org/10.1007/s00146-021-01375-x.

Coeckelbergh, M. (2023). Democracy, epistemic agency, and AI: Political epistemology in times of artificial intelligence. *AI Ethics*, 3(1), 1341–1350. https://doi.org/10.1007/s43681-022-00239-4.

Coeckelbergh, M., Sætra, H. S. (2023). Climate change and the political pathways of AI: The technocracy-democracy dilemma in light of artificial intelligence and human agency. *Technology in Society*, 75, 102406. https://doi.org/10.1016/j.techsoc.2023.102406.

Cohen, M. D., March, J. G., Olsen, J. P. (1972). A garbage can model of organizational choice. *Administrative Science Quarterly*, 17(1), 1–25.

Coles-Kemp, L., Ashenden, D., Morris, A., Yuille, J. (2022). Digital welfare: Designing for more nuanced forms of access. *Policy Design and Practice*, 3(2), 177–188. https://doi.org/10.1080/25741292.2020.1760414.

Collington, R. (2021). Disrupting the welfare state? Digitalisation and the retrenchment of public sector capacity. *New Political Economy*, 27(2), 312–328. https://doi.org/10.1080/13563467.2021.1952559.

Connolly, R. (2020). Why computing belongs within the social sciences. *Communications of the ACM*, 63(8), 54–59. https://doi.org/10.1145/3383444.

Cowls, J., Tsamados, A., Taddeo, M., Floridi, L. (2023). The AI gambit: leveraging artificial intelligence to combat climate change—opportunities, challenges, and recommendations. *AI & Society*, 38(2), 283–307. https://doi.org/10.1007/s00146-021-01294-x.

Cox, T. (2019). Muddling-through and deep learning for managing large-scale uncertain risks. *Journal of Benefit-Cost Analysis*, 10(2), 226–250. https://doi.org/10.1017/bca.2019.17.

Craft, J., Halligan, J. (2020). *Advising Governments in the Westminster Tradition: Policy Advisory Systems in Australia*. Cambridge: Cambridge University Press.

Craft, J., Head, B., Howlett, M. P. (2024). Expertise, policy advice, and policy advisory systems in an open, participatory, and populist era: New challenges to research and practice. *Australian Journal of Public Administration*, 83, 143–155. https://doi.org/10.1111/1467-8500.12630.

Craft, J., Howlett, M. P. (2013). The dual dynamics of policy advisory systems: The impact of externalization and politicization on policy advice. *Policy and Society*, 32(3), 187–197. https://doi.org/10.1016/j.polsoc.2013.07.001.

Crawford, K. (2021). *The Atlas of AI: Power, Politics, and the Planetary Costs of Artificial Intelligence*. New Haven: Yale University Press.

Cross, E., Ramsey, R. (2021). Minds meets machines: Towards a cognitive science of human-machine interactions. *Trends in Cognitive Sciences*, 25(3), 200–212. https://doi.org/10.1016/j.tics.2020.11.009.

Cugurullo, F., Caprotti, F., Cook, M., et al. (2023). The rise of AI urbanism in post-smart cities: A critical commentary on urban artificial intelligence. *Urban Studies*, 61(6), 1168–1182. https://doi.org/10.1177/00420980231203386.

Cugurullo, F., Xu, Y. (2025). When AIs become oracles: generative artificial intelligence, anticipatory urban governance, and the future of cities. *Policy and Society*, 44(1), 98–115. https://doi.org/10.1093/polsoc/puae025.

Curtis, C., Gillespie, N., Lockey, S. (2023). AI-deploying organizations are key to addressing 'perfect storm' of AI risks. *AI Ethics*, 3, 145–153. https://doi.org/10.1007/s43681-022-00163-7.

Das, D., Kwek, B. (2024). AI and data-driven urbanism: The Singapore experience. *Digital Geography and Society*, 7, 100104. https://doi.org/10.1016/j.diggeo.2024.100104.

Daugherty, P., Wilson, H. (2018). *Human + Machine: Reimagining Work in the Age of AI*. Boston: Harvard Business Press.

De Leon, P. (1981). Policy sciences: Discipline and profession. *Policy Sciences*, 13(1), 1–7.

DeSouza, K. C., Jacob, B. (2017). Big data in the public sector: Lessons for practitioners and scholars. *Administration & Society*, 49(7), 1043–1064. https://doi.org/10.1177/0095399714555751.

Deutsch, K. W. (1963). *The Nerves of Government. Models of Political Communication and Control*. New York: Free Press.

Diakopoulos, N., Johnson, D. (2021). Anticipating and addressing the ethical implications of deepfakes in the context of elections. *New Media & Society*, 23(7), 2072–2098. https://doi.org/10.1177/1461444820925811.

Domingos, P. (2015). *The Master Algorithm: How the Quest for the Ultimate Learning Machine Will Remake Our World*. New York: Basic Books.

Dunleavy, P. (2016). Big data and policy learning. *Evidence-Based Policy Making in the Social Sciences. Methods That Matter*. Edited by Stoker, Gerry, Evans, Mark. Chicago: Policy Press.

Dunleavy, P., Margetts, H. (2024). Data science, artificial intelligence and the third wave of digital era governance. *Public Policy and Administration*, 40(2), 185–214. https://doi.org/10.1177/09520767231198737.

Dunlop, C. (2016). Knowledge, epistemic communities and agenda-setting, in Zahariadis, N. (ed), *Routledge Handbook of Agenda-Setting*. London: Routledge, 273–295.

Dunlop, C. A. (2017). The irony of epistemic learning: Epistemic communities, policy learning and the case of Europe's hormones saga. *Policy and Society*, 36(2), 215–232. https://doi.org/10.1080/14494035.2017.1322260.

Dunlop, C. A., Radaelli, C. M. (2020). Policy Learning in comparative policy analysis. *Journal of Comparative Policy Analysis: Research and Practice*, 24(1), 51–72. https://doi.org/10.1080/13876988.2020.1762077.

Dwivedi, Y. K., Kshetri, N., Hughes, L., et al. (2023). Opinion paper: "So what if ChatGPT wrote it?" Multidisciplinary perspectives on opportunities, challenges and implications of generative conversational AI for research, practice and policy. *International Journal of Information Management*, 71, 102642. https://doi.org/10.1016/j.ijinfomgt.2023.102642.

Eisenstein, J. (2019). *Introduction to Natural Language Processing*. Cambridge, MA: MIT Press.

Elmore, R. F. (1979). Backward mapping: Implementation research and policy decisions. *Political Science Quarterly*, 94(4), 601–616.

Esko, T., Koulu, R. (2023). Imaginaries of better administration: Renegotiating the relationship between citizens and digital public power. *Big Data & Society*, 10(1), https://doi.org/10.1177/20539517231164113.

Estlund, D. (2008). *Democratic Authority: A Philosophical Framework*. Princeton: Princeton University Press.

Estrada, M. A. R. (2011). Policy modeling: Definition, classification and evaluation. *Journal of Policy Modeling*, 33(4), 523–536. https://doi.org/10.1016/j.jpolmod.2011.02.003.

Etzioni, A. (1968). *The Active Society. A Theory of Societal and Political Process*. New York: Free Press.

Eubanks, V. (2018). *Automating Inequality: How High-Tech Tools Profile, Police, and Punish the Poor*. New York: St. Martin's Press.

Filgueiras, F. (2022a). Big data, artificial intelligence and the future of regulatory tools, in Howlett, M. P. (ed.), *Routledge Handbook on Policy Tools*. London: Routledge, pp. 529–539.

Filgueiras, F. (2022b). New Pythias of public administration: Ambiguity and choice in AI systems as challenges for governance. *AI & Society*, 37(4), 1473–1486. https://doi.org/10.1007/s00146-021-01201-4.

Filgueiras, F., Almeida, V. (2021). *Governance for the Digital World: Neither More State Nor More Market*. London: Palgrave.

Fischer, F. (2016) What is critical? Connecting the policy analysis to political critique. *Critical Policy Studies*, 10(1), 95–98. https://doi.org/10.1080/19460171.2015.1129350.

Floridi, L. (2023a). AI as agency without intelligence: On ChatGPT, Large Language Models, and other generative models. *Philosophy & Technology*, 36(1), 15.

Floridi, L. (2023b). *The Ethics of Artificial Intelligence. Principles, Challenges and Opportunities*. Oxford: Oxford University Press.

Floridi, L. (2013). *The Philosophy of Information*. Oxford: Oxford University Press.

Forestal, J. (2022). *Designing for Democracy: How to Build Community in Digital Environments*. Oxford: Oxford University Press.

Frischmann, B., Selinger, E. (2018). *Re-engineering Humanity*. Cambridge: Cambridge University Press.

Gabriel, I. (2020). Artificial intelligence, values, and alignment. *Minds & Machines*, 30, 411–437. https://doi.org/10.1007/s11023-020-09539-2.

Gasser, U., Almeida, V. (2017). A layered model of AI goverance. *IEEE Internet Computing*, 21(6), 58–62. http://dx.doi.org/10.1109/MIC.2017.4180835.

Ghosh, A., Saini, A., Barad, H. (2025). Artificial intelligence in governance: Recent trends, risks, challenges, innovative frameworks and future directions. *AI & Society*, early view, 1–23. https://doi.org/10.1007/s00146-025-02312-y.

Giest, S. (2017). Big data for policymaking: fad or fasttrack? *Policy Analysis*, 50(3), 367–382. https://doi.org/10.1007/s11077-017-9293-1.

Gitelman, S. (2013). *Raw Data Is an Oxymoron*. Cambridge, MA: MIT Press.

Goldman, A. I. (2003). *The Technology and Economics of Communication, Knowledge in a Social World*. Oxford: Oxford University Press.

Gyódi, K., Nawaro, Ł., Paliński, M., Wilamowski, M. (2023). Informing policy with text mining: Technological change and social challenges. *Quality & Quantity*, 57, 933–954. https://doi.org/10.1007/s11135-022-01378-w.

Halligan, J. (1995). Policy advice and the public service, in Peters, B.G., Savoie, D. J. (eds.), *Governance in a Changing Environment*. Montreal: McGill-Queens' University Press and Canadian Centre for Management Development, pp. 138–172.

Hartley, K, Kuecker, G. D. (2022). *Disrupted Governance: Towards a New Policy Science*. Cambridge: Cambridge University Press.

Hashem, Y., Bright, J., Chakraborty, S., et al. (2025). Mapping the potential: Generative AI and public sector work. Using time use data to identify opportunities for AI adoption in Great Britain's public sector. London: The Alan Turing Institute. www.turing.ac.uk/news/publications/mapping-potential-generative-ai-and-public-sector-work-using-time-use-data.

Heclo, H. (1974). *Modern Social Politics in Britain and Sweden: From Relief to Income Maintenance*. New Haven: Yale University Press.

Hellström, T., Jacob, M. (2017). Policy instrument affordances: a framework for analysis. *Policy Studies*, 38(6), 604–621. https://doi.org/10.1080/01442872.2017.1386442.

Henman, P. (2018). Of algorithms, Apps and advice: Digital social policy and service delivery. *Journal of Asian Public Policy*, 12(1), 71–89. https://doi.org/10.1080/17516234.2018.1495885.

Hentenryck, P. (2021). Machine learning for optimal power flows. *Tutorials in Operations Research*, 5(4), 62–82. https://doi.org/10.1287/educ.2021.0234.

Hill, M., Hupe, P. (2009). *Implementing Public Policy*. Thousand Oaks: Sage.

Hjern, B., Porter, D. (1981). Implementation structures: A new unit of administrative analysis. *Organizational Studies*, 2(3), 211–227. https://doi.org/10.1177/017084068100200301.

Hong, S. (2024). AI and bias, in Paul, R., Carmel, E., Cobbe, J. (eds.), *Handbook on Public Policy and Artificial Intelligence*. Cheltenham: Edward-Elgar, 109–122.

Hood, C. C., Margetts, H. (2007). *The Tools of Government in Digital Age*. London: Palgrave MacMillan.

Howlett, M. P. (2019). *Policy design primer: Choosing the Right Tools for the Job*. London: Routledge.

Howlett, M. P. (2019). Procedural policy tools and the temporal dimensions of policy design. *International Review of Public Policy*, 1(1), 27–45. https://doi.org/10.4000/irpp.310.

Howlett, M. P. (2015). Policy analytical capacity: The supply and demand for policy analysis in government. *Policy and Society*, 34(3–4), 173–182. http://dx.doi.org/10.1016/j.polsoc.2015.09.002.

Howlett, M. P., Giest, S., Mukherjee, I., Taeihagh, A. (2025). New policy tools and traditional policy models: Better understanding behavioural, digital and collaborative instruments. *Policy Design and Practice*, 8(1), 121–137. https://doi.org/10.1080/25741292.2025.2495373.

Howlett, M. P., Mukherjee, I., Rayner, J. (2018). Understanding policy designs over time. In *Routledge Handbook of Policy Design*, edited by M. Howlett. London: Routledge.

Howlett, M. P., Ramesh, M. (2003). *Studying Public Policy. Policy Cycles and Policy Subsystems*. Oxford: Oxford University Press.

Hurley, M. W., Wallace, W. A. (1986). Expert systems as decision aids for public managers: An assessment of the technology and prototyping as a design strategy. *Public Administration Review*, 46(4), 563–571.

Ifenthaler, D., Majumdar, R., Gorissen, P. et al. (2024). Artificial intelligence in education: Implications for policymakers, researchers, and practitioners. *Technology, Knowledge and Learning*, early view, 1–18. https://doi.org/10.1007/s10758-024-09747-0.

Imperial, M. (2021). Implementation structures: The use of top-down and bottom-up approaches to policy implementation. *Oxford Research Encyclopedia – Politics*. https://doi.org/10.1093/acrefore/9780190228637.013.1750.

Innerarity, D. (2024). The epistemic impossibility of an artificial intelligence take-over of democracy. *AI & Society*, 39(4), 1667–1671. https://doi.org/10.1007/s00146-023-01632-1.

Jacobs, J. (2024). The artificial intelligence shock and socio-political polarization. *Technological Forecasting and Social Change*, 199, 123006. https://doi.org/10.1016/j.techfore.2023.123006.

Jaidka, K., Chen, T., Chesterman, S., et al. (2025). Misinformation, disinformation, and generative AI: Implications for perception and policy. *Digital Government Research & Practice*, 6(1), 1–15. https://doi.org/10.1145/3689372.

Janssen, M., Helbig, N. (2018). Innovating and changing the policy-cycle: Policy-makers be prepared! *Government Information Quarterly*, 35(1), 99–105. https://doi.org/10.1016/j.giq.2015.11.009.

Jarrahi, M. H., Lutz, C., Newlands, G. (2022). Artificial intelligence, human intelligence and hybrid intelligence based on mutual augmentation. *Big Data & Society*, 9(2), 1–6. https://doi.org/10.1177/20539517221142824.

Judge, B., Nitzberg, M, Russell, S. (2025). When code isn't law: Rethinking regulation for artificial intelligence. *Policy and Society*, 44(1), 85–97. https://doi.org/10.1093/polsoc/puae020.

Kahneman, D. (2003). Maps of bounded rationality: Psychology for behavioral economics. *American Economic Review*, 93(5), 1449–1475. https://doi.org/10.1257/000282803322655392.

Kayser-Bril, N. (2020). In a quest to optimize welfare management, Denmark built a surveillance behemoth. *Algorithmic Watch*. Retrieved from: In a quest to optimize welfare management, Denmark built a surveillance behemoth.

Khanal, S., Zhang, H., Taeihagh, A. (2025). Why and how is the power of Big Tech increasing in the policy process? The case of generative AI. *Policy and Society*, 44(1), 52–69. https://doi.org/10.1093/polsoc/puae012.

Kingdon, J. W. (1995). *Agendas, Alternatives, and Public Policies*. New York: Harper & Collins.

Kitchin, R. (2014). *The Data Revolution: Big Data, Open Data, Data Infrastructures and Their Consequences*. Thousand Oaks: Sage.

Klijn, E. H., & Koppenjan, J. (2012). Governance network theory: Past, present, and future. *Policy and Politics*, 40(4), 587–606. https://doi.org/10.1332/030557312x655431.

Knorr-Cetina, K. (1999). *Epistemic Cultures: How the Sciences Make Knowledge*. Cambridge, MA: Harvard University Press.

Koga, N. M., Palotti, P. L. M, Pontes, P. A. M. M., Couto, B. G., Soares, M. L. V. (2023). Analytical capacity as a critical condition for responding to COVID-19 in Brazil. *Policy and Society*, 42(1), 117–130. https://doi.org/10.1093/polsoc/puac028.

König, P. D., Wenzelburger, G. (2020). Opportunity for renewal or disruptive force? How artificial intelligence alters democratic politics. *Government Information Quarterly*, 37(3), 101489. https://doi.org/10.1016/j.giq.2020.101489.

Korinek, A., Balwit, A. (2023). Aligned with whom? Direct and social goals and AI systems, in Bullock, J. B., Chen, Y. C., Himmelreich, J. et al. (eds.), *The Oxford handbook of AI governance*. Oxford: Oxford University Press, 65–85.

Krishnamoorthy, C. S., Rajeev, S. (1996). *Artificial Intelligence and Expert Systems for Engineers*. Boca Raton: CRC Press.

Lazar, S. (2024). Automatic authorities: Power and AI, in Lane, M., Sethumadhavan, A. (eds.), *Collaborative Intelligence: How Humans and AI are Transforming our World*. Cambridge, MA: MIT Press, 32–45.

Landemore, H. (2012). *Democratic Reason: Politics, Collective Intelligence, and the Rule of Many*. Princeton: Princeton University Press.

Lascoumes, P., Le Galès, P. (2007). Understanding public policy thorough its instruments – From the nature of instruments to the sociology of public policy instrumentation. *Governance*, 20(1), 1–21. https://doi.org/10.1111/j.1468-0491.2007.00342.x.

Lasswell, H. D. (1970). The emerging conception of policy sciences. *Policy Sciences*, 1(1), 3–14.

LeCun, Y., Bengio, Y, Hinton, G. (2015). Deep learning. *Nature*, 521, 436–444. https://doi.org/10.1038/nature14539.

Lehdonvirta, V. (2024). *Cloud Empires: How Digital Platforms Are Overtaking the State and How We Can Regain Control*. Cambridge, MA: MIT Press.

Lim, H. S. M., Taeihagh, A. (2019). Algorithmic decision-making in AVs: Understanding ethical and technical concerns for smart cities. *Sustainability*, 11(20), 5791. https://doi.org/10.3390/su11205791.

Lin, T. C. W. (2017). The new market manipulation. *Emory Law Journal*, 66(6), 1253–1314.

Lindblom, C. E. (1959). The science of muddling through. *Public Administration Review*, 19(2), 79–88.

Lipsky, M. (2010). *Street-Level Bureaucracy: Dilemmas of the Individual in Public Service*. New York: Russell Sage Foundation.

Liu, H. K., Tang, M., Collard, A. S. J. (2025). Hybrid intelligence for the public sector: A bibliometric analysis of artificial intelligence and crowd intelligence. *Government Information Quarterly*, 42(1), 102006. https://doi.org/10.1016/j.giq.2024.102006.

Liu, M., Zhang, H., Sui, Y. (2024). Workplace artificial intelligence regulation in China: Between efficiency and social stability. *ILR Review*, 77 (5), 813–824. https://doi.org/10.1177/00197939241278956b.

Logan, S. (2024). Tell me what you don't know: Large language models and the pathologies of intelligence analysis. *Australian Journal of International Affairs*, 78(2), 220–228. https://doi.org/10.1080/10357718.2024.2331733.

Lowi, T. (1964). American business, public policy, case-studies, and political theory. *World Politics*, 16(4), 677–715. https://doi.org/10.2307/2009452.

Maragno, G., Tangi, L., Gastaldi, L., Benedetti, M. (2023). Exploring the factors, affordances and constraints outlining the implementation of artificial intelligence in public sector organizations. *International Journal of Information Management*, 73, 102686. https://doi.org/10.1016/j.ijinfomgt.2023.102686.

Margetts, H., John, P. (2024). How rediscovering nodality can improve democratic governance in digital world. *Public Administration*, 102(3), 969–983. https://doi.org/10.1111/padm.12960.

Margetts, H., Dorobantu, C. (2019). Rethink government with AI. *Nature*, 568(7751), 163–165.

Markram, H. (2006). The Blue Brain Project. *Nature Reviews Neuroscience*, 17(2), 153–160. https://doi.org/10.1038/nrn1848.

McCarthy, J. (1981). Epistemological problems of artificial intelligence, in Webber, B. L., Nilsson, N. I. (eds.), *Readings in Artificial Intelligence*. Berlin: Springer, pp. 459–465.

Meijer, A., Wessels, M. (2019). Predictive policing: Review of benefits and drawbacks. *International Journal of Public Administration*, 42(12), 1031–1039. https://doi.org/10.1080/01900692.2019.1575664.

Mendonça, R. F., Filgueiras, F., Almeida, V. A. (2023). *Algorithmic Institutionalism: The Changing Rules of Social + Political Life*. Oxford: Oxford University Press.

Mergel, I., Dickinson, H., Stenvall, J., Gasco, M. (2023). Implementing AI in the public sector. *Public Management Review*, early view, 1–14. https://doi.org/10.1080/14719037.2023.2231950.

Minsky, M. (1985). *The Society of Mind*. New York: Simon and Schuster.

Mökander, J., Schroeder, R. (2024). Artificial Intelligence, rationalization, and the limits of control in the public sector: The case of tax policy optimization. *Social Science Computer Review*, 42(6), 1359–1378. https://doi.org/10.1177/08944393241235175.

Moradi, M., Moradi, M., Bayat, F., Toosi, A. N. (2019). Collective hybrid intelligence: Towards a conceptual framework. *International Journal of Crowd Science*, 3(2), 198–220. https://doi.org/10.1108/IJCS-03-2019-0012.

Muccione, V., Vaghefi, S. A., Bingler, J. *et al.* (2024). Integrating artificial intelligence with expert knowledge in global environmental assessments: Opportunities, challenges and the way ahead. *Regional Environmental Change*, 24(121), 1–8. https://doi.org/10.1007/s10113-024-02283-8.

Neumann, O., Guirguis, K., Steiner, R. (2022). Exploring artificial intelligence adoption in public organizations: A comparative case study. *Public*

Management Review, 26(1), 114–141. https://doi.org/10.1080/14719037.2022.2048685.

Newman, J., Mintrom, M. (2023). Mapping the discourse on evidence-based policy, artificial intelligence, and the ethical practice of policy analysis. *Journal of European Public Policy*, 30(9),1839–1859. https://doi.org/10.1080/13501763.2023.2193223.

Nobel, S. U. (2018). *Algorithms of Oppression: How Search Engines Reinforce Racism*. New York: New York University Press.

Nowak, A. J. (2022). Artificial intelligence in evidence-based medicine, in Lidströmer N., Ashrafian, H. (eds.), *Artificial Intelligence in Medicine*. Berlin: Springer, 255–266. https://doi.org/10.1007/978-3-030-64573-1_43.

Nowotny, H. (2021). *In AI We Trust: Power, Illusion, and Control of Predictive Algorithms*. New York: Polity Books.

Oder, N., Béland, D. (2025). Artificial intelligence, emotional labor, and the quest for sociological and political imagination among low-skilled workers. *Policy and Society*, 44(1), 116–128. https://doi.org/10.1093/polsoc/puae034.

OECD. (2024). Governing with Artificial Intelligence: Are governments ready?, *OECD Artificial Intelligence Papers*, 20, OECD Publishing. https://doi.org/10.1787/26324bc2-en.

Olsen, J. P. (2006). Maybe it is time to rediscover bureaucracy. *Journal of Public Administration Research and Theory*, 16(1), 1–24. https://doi.org/10.1093/jopart/mui027.

O'Neil, C. (2016). *The Weapons of Math Destruction: How Big Data Increases Inequality and Threatens Democracy*. New York: Crown.

Ostrom, E. (2005). *Understanding Institutional Diversity*. Princeton: Princeton University Press.

Padmaja, B., Moorthy, C. V. K. N. S. N., Venkateswarulu, N., Bala, M. M. (2023). Exploration of issues, challenges and latest developments in autonomous cars. *Journal of Big Data*, 10, 1–24. https://doi.org/10.1186/s40537-023-00701-y.

Pattyn, V., Brans, M. (2015). Organisational analytical capacity: Policy evaluation in Belgium. *Policy and Society*, 34(3–4), 183–196. https://doi.org/10.1016/j.polsoc.2015.09.009.

Paul, R. (2022). Can critical policy studies outsmart AI? Research agenda on artificial intelligence technologies and public policy. *Critical Policy Studies*, 16(4), 497–509. https://doi.org/10.1080/19460171.2022.2123018.

Pedreschi, D., Pappalardo, L., Ferragina, E., et al. (2025). Human-AI coevolution. *Artificial Intelligence*, 339, 104244. https://doi.org/10.1016/j.artint.2024.104244.

Peeters, R., Rentería, C., Cejudo, G. M. (2023). How information capacity shapes policy implementation: A comparison of administrative burdens in COVID-19 vaccination programs in the United States, Mexico, and the Netherlands. *Government Information Quarterly*, 40(4), 101871. https://doi.org/10.1016/j.giq.2023.101871.

Peters, B. G., Pierre, J. (2016). *Comparative Governance: Rediscovering the Functional Dimension of Governing.* Cambridge: Cambridge University Press.

Peters, B. G. (2012). Information and governing: Cybernetic models of governance, in Levi-Faur, D. (ed.), *The Oxford Handbook of Governance.* Oxford: Oxford University Press, 113–128.

Pressman, J. L., Wildavsky, A. (1984). *Implementation.* Berkeley: University of California Press.

Ramezani, M., Takian, A., Bakhtiari, A. et al. (2023). The application of artificial intelligence in health policy: A scoping review. *BMC Health Services Research*, 23, 1416. https://doi.org/10.1186/s12913-023-10462-2.

Reid, T., Gibert, J. (2022). Inclusion in human-machines interactions. *Science*, 375(6577), 149–150. https://doi.org/10.1126/science.abf2618.

Rikap, C. (2021). *Capitalism, Power and Innovation.* London: Routledge.

Russell, S. (2022). Why we need to regulate non-state use of arms. *Forum Institutional.* 18 May. www.weforum.org/agenda/2022/05/regulate-non-state-use-arms/#:~:text=Stuart%20Russell&text=An%20emerging%20arms%20race%20between,while%20the%20technology%20rapidly%20advances.

Russell, S. J. (2019). *Human Compatible: Artificial Intelligence and the Problem of Control.* New York: Viking Books.

Russell, S. J., Norvig, P. (2010). *Artificial Intelligence: A Modern Approach.* Englewood Cliffs: Prentice-Hall.

Sabatier, P. A. (1999). The need for better theories, in Sabatier, P. A. (ed.), *Theories of the Policy Process.* Boulder: Westview, pp. 3–17.

Sætra, H. S. (2023). The promise and pitfalls of techno-solutionism, in *Technology and Sustainable Development: The Promises and Pitfalls of Techno-solutionism.* London: Routledge, 1–9.

Safaei, M., Longo, J. (2024). The end of policy analyst? Testing the capability of artificial intelligence to generate plausible, persuasive and useful policy analysis. *Digital Government: Research and Practice*, 5(1), 4–35. https://doi.org/10.1145/3604570.

Salamon, L. (2002). *The tools of Government: A Guide to the New Governance.* Oxford: Oxford University Press.

Samuel, A. L. (1962). Artificial intelligence: A frontier of automation. *The Annals of the American Academy of Political and Social Science*, 340(1), 10–20. https://doi.org/10.1177/000271626234000103.

Samuel, A. (1959). Some studies in machine learning using the game of checkers. *IBM Journal of Research and Development*, 44(1.2), 210–229. https://doi.org/10.1147/rd.33.0210.

Schlosser, M. (2019). Agency, in Zalta E. N. (ed.), *The Stanford Encyclopedia of Philosophy*. Stanford: Stanford University, 1–8. www.plato.stanford.edu/archives/win2019/entries/agency/.

Schrage, M. (2020). *Recommendation Engines*. Cambridge, MA: MIT Press.

Schuett, J. (2023). Risk management in the artificial intelligence act. *European Journal of Risk Regulation*, 15(2), 367–385. https://doi.org/10.1017/err.2023.1.

Schwember, H. (1977). Cybernetics in government: Experience with new tools for management in Chile 1971–1973. In Bossel, H. (ed.), *Concepts and Tools of Computer-Assisted Policy Analysis: Vol. 1: Basic Concepts*. Birkhäuser: Basel, pp. 79–138.

Searle, J. R. (1980). Minds, brains, and programs. *Behavioral and Brain Sciences*, 3(3), 417–424. https://doi.org/10.1017/S0140525X00005756.

Shardlow, M., Przybila, P. (2023). Deanthropomorphising NLP: Can a Language Model Be Conscious? *ArXiv*, 1–20. https://doi.org/10.48550/arXiv.2211.11483.

Siddiki, S. (2020). *Understanding and Analyzing Public Policy Design*. Cambridge: Cambridge University Press.

Silva, E. H. M., Santos, E. M. F., Miranda, M. L. B. M., Bezerra, S. L., Miranda, S. C. (2024). ChatTCU: Inteligência artificial como assistente do auditor. *Revista do TCU*, 153, 19–45.

Simon, H. A. (1947). *Administrative Behavior*. New York: Free Press.

Simon, H. A. (1970). *The Sciences of Artificial*. Cambridge, MA: MIT Press.

Simon, H. A. (1983). *Reason in Human Affairs*. Stanford: Stanford University Press.

Simon, H. A. (1995). Artificial intelligence: An empirical science. *Artificial Intelligence*, 77(1) 95–127.

Simon, H. A., Eisenstadt, S. A. (2002). A Chinese room that understands, in Bishop, J. M., Preston, J. (eds.), *Views into the Chinese Room: New Essays on Searle and Artificial Intelligence*. Oxford: Oxford University Press, 95–108.

Song, S., Liu, X., Li, Y., Yu, Y. (2022). Pandemic policy assessment by artificial intelligence. *Nature – Scientific Reports*, 12, 13843. https://doi.org/10.1038/s41598-022-17892-8.

Sorensen, E., Torfing, J. (2005). The democratic anchorage of governance networks. *Scandinavian Political Studies*, 28(3), 195–218. https://doi.org/10.1111/j.1467-9477.2005.00129.x.

Simon, H. A. (1957). *The Models of Man*. New York: John Wiley & Sons.

Simons, A., Voß, J. P. (2018). The concept of instrument constituencies: Accounting for dynamics and practices of knowing governance. *Policy and Society*, 37(1), 14–35. https://doi.org/10.1080/14494035.2017.1375248.

Stoker, G. (1998). Governance as theory: Five propositions. *International Social Science Journal*, 50(155), 17–28. https://doi.org/10.1111/1468-2451.00106.

Straub, V. J., Morgan, D., Bright, J., Margetts, H. (2023). Artificial intelligence in government: Concepts, standards, and a unified framework. *Government Information Quarterly*, 40(4), 101881. https://doi.org/10.1016/j.giq.2023.101881.

Suchman, L. (2007). *Human-Machine Reconfigurations: Plans and Situated Actions*. Cambridge: Cambridge University Press.

Sun, T. Q., Medaglia, R. (2019). Mapping the challenges of Artificial Intelligence in the public sector: Evidence from public healthcare. *Government Information Quarterly*, 36(2), 368–383. https://doi.org/10.1016/j.giq.2018.09.008.

Süsser, D., Ceglarz, A., Gaschnig, H., et al. (2021). Model-based policymaking or policy-based modelling? How energy models and energy policy interact. *Energy Research & Social Science*, 75, 101984. https://doi.org/10.1016/j.erss.2021.101984.

Sutton, R., Barto, A. (2018). *Introduction to Reinforcement Learning*. Cambridge, MA: MIT Press.

Taeihagh, A. (2025). Governance of generative AI. *Policy and Society*, 44(1), 1–22. https://doi.org/10.1093/polsoc/puaf001.

Taeihagh, A., Ramesh, M., Howlett, M. (2021). Assessing the regulatory challenges of emerging disruptive technologies. *Regulation & Governance*, 15(4), 1009–1019. https://doi.org/10.1111/rego.12392.

Tallberg, J., Erman, E., Furendal, M., et al. (2023). The global governance of artificial intelligence: Next steps for empirical and normative research. *International Studies Review*, 25(3), viad040. https://doi.org/10.1093/isr/viad040.

Tomasello, M. (2022). *The Evolution of Agency: Behavioral Organizations from Lizards to Humans*. Cambridge, MA: MIT Press.

Turing, A. (1950). Computing Machinery and Intelligence. *Mind—A Quarterly Review of Psychology and Philosophy*, 59(236), 433–460.

Turkle, S. (1984). *The Second Self: Computers and the Human Spirit*. New York: Simon & Schuster.

Tyler, C., Akerlof, K. L., Allegra, A., et al. (2023). AI tools as science policy advisers? The potential and the pitfalls. *Nature*, 622, 27–30. https://doi.org/10.1038/d41586-023-02999-3.

Ulnicane, I. (2022). Artificial intelligence in the European Union, in Hoerber, T, Weber, G., Cabras, I. (eds.), *The Routledge Handbook on European Integrations*. London: Routledge, 95–108. https://doi.org/10.4324/9780429262081-19.

Ulnicane, I., Aden, A. (2023). Power and politics in framing bias in Artificial Intelligence policy. *Review of Policy Research*, 40(5), 665–687. https://doi.org/10.1111/ropr.12567.

Urbina, F., Lentzos, F., Invernizzi, C., Ekins, S. (2022). Dual use of artificial-intelligence-powered drug discovery. *Nature Machine Intelligence*, 4, 189–191. https://doi.org/10.1038/s42256-022-00465-9.

Valle-Cruz, D., Fernandez-Cortez, V., Gil-Garcia, J. R. (2022). From E-budgeting to smart budgeting: Exploring the potential of artificial intelligence in government decision-making for resource allocation. *Government Information Quarterly*, 39(2), 101644. https://doi.org/10.1016/j.giq.2021.101644.

Valle-Cruz, D., Sandoval-Almazán, R. (2022). Role and governance of artificial intelligence in the public policy cycle, in Justin B., Bullock et al. (eds.), *The Oxford Handbook of AI Governance*. Oxford: Oxford University Press, 534–550.

Valle-Cruz, D., Criado, J. I., Sandoval-Almazán, R., Ruvalcaba-Gomez, E. A. (2020). Assessing the public policy-cycle framework in the age of artificial intelligence: From agenda-setting to policy evaluation. *Government Information Quarterly*, 37(4), 101509. https://doi.org/10.1016/j.giq.2020.101509.

Van der Voort, H. G., Klievink, A. J., Arnaboldi, M., Meijer, A. J. (2019). Rationality and politics of algorithms: Will the promise of big data survive the dynamics of public decision making? *Government Information Quarterly*, 36(1), 27–38. https://doi.org/10.1016/j.giq.2018.10.011.

van Prooijen, J. W., Šrol, J., Maglić, M. (2025). How belief in conspiracy theories could harm sustainability. *Nature Human Behavior*, early view. https://doi.org/10.1038/s41562-025-02243-0.

Veale, M., Brass, I. (2019). Administration by algorithm? Public management meets public sector machine learning, in Yeung. K, Lodge, M. (eds), *Algorithmic Regulation*. Oxford: Oxford University Press, 121–149. https://doi.org/10.1093/oso/9780198838494.003.0006.

Vedung, E. (2009). *Public Policy and Program Evaluation*. New Brunswick: Transaction.

Verhulst, S. G. (2018). Where and when AI and CI meet: Exploring the intersection of artificial and collective intelligence towards the goal of innovating how we govern. *AI & Society*, 33(2), 293–297. https://doi.org/10.1007/s00146-018-0830-z.

Veselý, A. (2017). Policy advice as policy work: A conceptual framework for multi-level analysis. *Policy Sciences*, 50, 139–154. https://doi.org/10.1007/s11077-016-9255-z.

Vial, G. (2019). Understanding digital transformation: A review and a research agenda. *The Journal of Strategic Information Systems*, 28(2), 118–144. https://doi.org/10.1016/j.jsis.2019.01.003.

Voß, J.-P., Simons, A. (2014). Instrument constituencies and the supply side of policy innovation: The social life of emissions trading. *Environmental Politics*, 23(5), 735–754. https://doi.org/10.1080/09644016.2014.923625.

Wang, P. (2019). On defining artificial intelligence. *Journal of General Artificial Intelligence*, 10(2), 1–37. https://doi.org/10.2478/jagi-2019-0002.

Wang, H., Fu, T., Du, Y. et al. (2023). Scientific discovery in the age of artificial intelligence. *Nature*, 620, 47–60. https://doi.org/10.1038/s41586-023-06221-2.

Wani, A.K., Rahayu, F., Ben Amor, I. et al. (2024). Environmental resilience through artificial intelligence: Innovations in monitoring and management. *Environmental Science Pollution Research*, 31, 18379–18395. https://doi.org/10.1007/s11356-024-32404-z.

Weiss, C. H. (1998). Have we learned anything new about the use of evaluation? *American Journal of Evaluation*, 19(1), 21–33. https://doi.org/10.1016/S1098-2140(99)80178-7.

Weiss, C. H. (1979). *Using Social Research in Public Policy Making*. London: Lexington Books.

Weizenbaum, J. (1976). *Computer Power and Human Reason: From Judgment to Calculation*. San Francisco: W. H. Freeman.

White House (2023). Executive order on the safe, secure, and trustworthy development and use of Artificial Intelligence. www.whitehouse.gov/briefing-room/presidential-actions/2023/10/30/executive-order-on-the-safe-secure-and-trustworthy-development-and-use-of-artificial-intelligence/?utm_source=link.

Willems, J., Schmidthuber, L., Vogel, D., Ebinger, F., & Vanderelst, D. (2022). Ethics of robotized public services: The role of robot design and its actions. *Government Information Quarterly*, 39(2). https://doi.org/10.1016/j.giq.2022.101683.

Wilson, R. (2009). Policy analysis as policy advice, in Goodin, R. E., Moran, M., Rein, M. (eds.), *The Oxford Handbook of Public Policy*. Oxford University Press, 152–168.

Wirtz, B. W., Weyerer, J. C., Sturm, B. J. (2020). The dark sides of artificial intelligence: An integrated AI governance framework for public administration. *International Journal of Public Administration*, 43(9), 818–829. https://doi.org/10.1080/01900692.2020.1749851.

Xavier, B. (2025). Biases within AI: Challenging the illusion of neutrality. *AI & Society*, 40, 1545–1546. https://doi.org/10.1007/s00146-024-01985-1.

Yang, Q., Wu, K., Jiang, Y. (2007). Learning action models from plan examples using weighted MAX-SAT. *Artificial Intelligence*, 171(2), 107–143. https://doi.org/10.1016/j.artint.2006.11.005.

Yeung, K. (2018). Algorithmic regulation: A critical interrogation. *Regulation & Governance*, 12(4), 505–523. https://doi.org/10.1111/rego.12158.

Yoshida, Y., Sitas, N., Mannetti,L., et al. (2024). Beyond academia: A case for reviews of gray literature for science-policy processes and applied research. *Environmental Science & Policy*, 162, 103882. https://doi.org/10.1016/j.envsci.2024.103882.

Yuwono, E. I., Tjondronegoro, D., Riverola, C., Loy, J. (2024). Co-creation in action: Bridging the knowledge gap in artificial intelligence among innovation champions. *Computers and Education: Artificial Intelligence*, 7, 100272. https://doi.org/10.1016/j.caeai.2024.100272.

Zakharova, I., Jarke, J., Kaun, A. (2024). Tensions in digital welfare states: Three perspectives on care and control. *Journal of Sociology*, 60(3), 540–559.

Zhou, Z. H. (2012). *Ensemble Methods: Foundations and Algorithms*. New York: CRC Press.

Zhuo, H. H., Yang, Q., Hu, D. H., Li, L. (2010). Learning complex action models with quantifiers and logical implications. *Artificial Intelligence*, 174(18), 1540–1569. https://doi.org/10.1016/j.artint.2010.09.007.

Cambridge Elements

Public Policy

M. Ramesh
National University of Singapore (NUS)

M. Ramesh is UNESCO Chair on Social Policy Design at the Lee Kuan Yew School of Public Policy, NUS. His research focuses on governance and social policy in East and Southeast Asia, in addition to public policy institutions and processes. He has published extensively in reputed international journals. He is co-editor of *Policy and Society* and *Policy Design and Practice*.

Michael Howlett
Simon Fraser University, British Columbia

Michael Howlett is Burnaby Mountain Professor and Canada Research Chair (Tier1) in the Department of Political Science, Simon Fraser University. He specialises in public policy analysis, and resource and environmental policy. He is currently editor-in-chief of *Policy Sciences* and co-editor of the *Journal of Comparative Policy Analysis, Policy and Society* and *Policy Design and Practice*.

Xun WU
Hong Kong University of Science and Technology (Guangzhou)

Xun WU is currently a Professor at the Innovation, Policy and Entrepreneurship Thrust at the Society Hub of Hong Kong University of Science and Technology (Guangzhou). He is a policy scientist with a strong interest in the linkage between policy analysis and public management. Trained in engineering, economics, public administration, and policy analysis, his research seeks to make contribution to the design of effective public policies in dealing emerging policy challenges across Asian countries.

Judith Clifton
University of Cantabria

Judith Clifton is Professor of Economics at the University of Cantabria, Spain, and Editor-in-Chief of *Journal of Economic Policy Reform*. Her research interests include the determinants and consequences of public policy across a wide range of public services, from infrastructure to health, particularly in Europe and Latin America, as well as public banks, especially, the European Investment Bank. Most recently, she is principal investigator on the Horizon Europe Project GREENPATHS (www.greenpaths.info) on the just green transition.

Eduardo Araral
National University of Singapore (NUS)

Eduardo Araral specializes in the study of the causes and consequences of institutions for collective action and the governance of the commons. He is widely published in various journals and books and has presented in more than ninety conferences. Ed was a 2021–22 Fellow at the Center for Advanced Study of Behavioral Sciences, Stanford University. He has received more than US$6.6 million in external research grants as the lead or co-PI for public agencies and corporations. He currently serves as a Special Issue Editor (collective action, commons, institutions, governance) for World Development and is a member of the editorial boards of *Water Economics and Policy, World Development Sustainability, Water Alternatives* and the *International Journal of the Commons*.

About the Series

Elements in Public Policy is a concise and authoritative collection of assessments of the state of the art and future research directions in public policy research, as well as substantive new research on key topics. Edited by leading scholars in the field, the series is an ideal medium for reflecting on and advancing the understanding of critical issues in the public sphere. Collectively, the series provides a forum for broad and diverse coverage of all major topics in the field while integrating different disciplinary and methodological approaches.

Cambridge Elements

Public Policy

Elements in the Series

Making Policy in a Complex World
Paul Cairney, Tanya Heikkila and Matthew Wood

Pragmatism and the Origins of the Policy Sciences: Rediscovering Lasswell and the Chicago School
William N. Dunn

The Protective State
Christopher Ansell

How Ideas and Institutions Shape the Politics of Public Policy
Daniel Béland

Policy Entrepreneurs and Dynamic Change
Michael Mintrom

Making Global Policy
Diane Stone

Understanding and Analyzing Public Policy Design
Saba Siddiki

Zombie Ideas: Why Failed Policy Ideas Persist
Brainard Guy Peters and Maximilian Lennart Nagel

Defining Policy Analysis: A Journey that Never Ends
Beryl A. Radin

Integrating Logics in the Governance of Emerging Technologies: The Case of Nanotechnology
Derrick Mason Anderson and Andrew Whitford

Truth and Post-Truth in Public Policy
Frank Fischer

Disrupted Governance: Towards a New Policy Science
Kris Hartley and Glen David Kuecker

Artificial Intelligence and Public Policy
Fernando Filgueiras

A full series listing is available at: www.cambridge.org/EPPO

For EU product safety concerns, contact us at Calle de José Abascal, 56–1°,
28003 Madrid, Spain or eugpsr@cambridge.org.

www.ingramcontent.com/pod-product-compliance
Lightning Source LLC
LaVergne TN
LVHW011853060526
838200LV00054B/4299